LIVING DISTINGUISHED

LEAVING YOUR FINGERPRINT ON THE WORLD

JEREMY & CONSUELA ROACH

Foreword by Bishop Joseph W. Walker, III
Presiding Bishop, Full Gospel Baptist Church International

Johnson, Bill. "Heaven Invades Earth." Treasure House. Destiny Image Publishers, Inc. P.O. Box 310 Shippensburg, PA. 17257-0310. 2003.

Richards, James B. "How to Stop the Pain." Whitaker House. 1030 Hunt Valley Circle. New Kensington, PA. 15068. 2001.

Bevere, John. "Relentless." WaterBrook Press. 12265 Oracle Boulevard, Suite 200. Colorado Springs, Colorado. 80921. 2011.

Richards, James B. "Grace: The Power to Change." Whitaker House. 1030 Hunt Valley Circle. New Kensington, PA. 15068. 1993.

Willis Jr, Avery T. "Master Life: Developing a Rich Personal Relationship with the Master." Broadman & Holman Publishers. Nashville, TN. 1998.

Tozer, A.W. "In the Pursuit of God." Published by Christian Publications, Inc. Camp Hills, PA, USA. 1991.

Photography by Tiffany Tann.

www.xulonpress.com

This book is dedicated to our sons, Landon Jeremyah and Langston Joshua. God blessed us with so much joy! Daddy and Mommy are so proud to be your parents and love you so much!

In memory of our precious Mother, Niokie Greene. We love and miss you!

Our Prayers

Thanksgiving Prayer To God

Heavenly Father, we acknowledge you, the power of the Holy Spirit within us and the finished work of Jesus on the Cross. Your grace has sustained us. Your anointing has equipped us. Your Spirit has led us. Your Son has redeemed us. For this we are eternally grateful, be glorified, in Jesus' name!

Prayer For The Reader

A prayer to pray as you journey through this book:

Heavenly Father, I pray that you will cause my heart to become open, receptive, and fertile to the truths of your Word. Bring my mind into alignment with the mind of Christ and renew and transform my life. Remove every distraction and bring clarity during my time of reading. Tune my ears to hear your voice and help me to receive your love, grace and the finished works of Jesus. Help me to understand, comprehend, retain and share with others the revelation that I shall receive. Lastly, Lord, cause me to draw closer to you as I partake of your Good news on each page, in Jesus name, Amen!

Contents

FOREWORD

We are living in radical times. Radical times require radical responses. This book challenges us all to live beyond complacency and take our rightful place as Kingdom representatives in the earth. The church has been guilty of prophetic laryngitis and not distinguishing itself amidst a rapid moral decline. We must realize the urgency of the times and be willing to live our lives as true disciples of Jesus Christ.

Many are searching for answers, and the world is providing them temporary solutions. The distinguished life is one of intentionality and spiritual fortitude. When we point people to Jesus Christ, we point them to the answer for the world today. Jeremy and Consuela have masterfully penned a book that not only inspires us but challenges us to be who God intended us to be in the world. The kingdom is in need of those like the three Hebrew boys who refused to bow down or Stephen, who stood for righteousness in the face of immeasurable consequences. The faith of those in times past is needed now more than ever. We are not called to be popular; rather we are called to make a difference in the lives of those who are lost.

This book is necessary, and I highly recommend it to you. Each chapter will equip you with the tools necessary to transform your life and the lives of others. Every day you go to work or school your willingness to live a distinguished life will make a difference. When you adopt these practical principles, you will impact the world in ways you never imagined.

The sacrifice of Jesus on the cross means nothing if we don't point people toward it. We must show them the love of Jesus Christ and allow them to experience redemption as we have. His word to us was to "go" and make disciples. We were not to just be disciples but to reproduce others who would spread this good news around the world. This call summons us all out of the comfort of our sanctuaries and commits us to the essence of our Christian faith.

I am so incredibly proud of Jeremy and Consuela. As their Pastor, I've seen them personify the distinguished life every day. This book is not just a "what you should do" but it's a guide to help you walk out the true meaning of being a disciple of Jesus Christ. The passion and prayer life of these two permeates each page, and I know it will encourage millions around the world. If you are serious about living a life of Christ and not just existing, this book is for you. If you are struggling with purpose, this book will put you on a path because all purpose begins with us fulfilling God's will in the earth. I highly recommend it to you and pray you, like me, are encouraged to do more and truly live the Distinguished Life.

Bishop Joseph Warren Walker, III
Senior Pastor, Mount Zion Baptist Church, Nashville, TN
Presiding Bishop, Full Gospel Baptist Church Fellowship International

FOREWORD

The Word of our Lord is an enduring Sword; it is eternal, and it will stand the test of time. "By their fruits, you will know them," says our Lord.

Over half a decade ago, I met Jeremy and Consuela when I assumed the deanship of Minister in Training (coded MIT) of Mt. Zion Baptist Church, where Bishop Joseph Warren Walker, III is the senior pastor. When I met them, I never knew they were courting each other. However, one thing I recognized in both of them was a willingness to submit to constituted authority. Both of them are living examples of a Christ-like spirit. I listened to them in class, and I concluded that they have had an encounter with the Lord Jesus Christ. After their training at MIT, I retained them to be instructors, and Consuela is the director of enrollment. They possess a mien of authority in their respective classes.

Finally, they decided to tie the knot through holy matrimony, and they asked me to help them in premarital counseling, and I gladly acceded to their request. Even during counseling time, their knowledge of the truth about Jesus Christ was not wanting. Watching both of them grow in grace is a blessing. They are now four and counting in the family. I know these two are destined to disgrace and degrade Satan, in the name of Jesus Christ.

They both approached me to write a foreword to their first book, and because I know them, that they are born again, both of them are serving elders at Mt. Zion Baptist Church, and members of instructional staff in MIT, I gladly accepted to do it. Their life is an epitome of what a Christian should be.

Now listen to me, dear reader of this book, Elders Jeremy and Consuela deserve to be heard. They are not theorist in the area they wrote about; they are pragmatists and authentic Christians. The book, *Living Distinguished* is crisp, lucid and heart penetrating. Reading the manuscript is like tasting honey. It is deep and transforming. Just like the honey that Jonathan tasted altered his countenance, so is this book. It will send sparkles in your face. It will touch you (1 Samuel 14:27). May this book stir up the minds of saints in our generation and the coming ones. God bless you.

Rev. Dr. Gideon A. Olaleye
Senior Pastor, New Beautiful Gate Church
and Ministries, Antioch, Tennessee
Dean, Ministers-In-Training Program,
Mount Zion Baptist Church, Nashville Tennessee

FOREWORD

Congratulations! You made a wise choice in what will now be a step in revolutionizing your life and relationships with God and people. Have you been wondering how on earth do you apply your faith to real life? Did someone introduce you to God but you can't figure out what is supposed to be different? Or maybe you have walked with the Lord for years but feel something is missing.

Jeremy and Consuela have laid out for you a journey of faith and transformation. You will want to read this multiple times as you begin to grow, truly living distinguished. Jesus distinguishes you, my friend! Truly, He has purpose and provision for you. There is no limit to His grace and His presence as you learn to walk more intimately with Jesus, are empowered by the Holy Spirit, and live Heaven on earth as you apply Kingdom living to your life right now.

Jeremy and Consuela Roach, in *Living Distinguished*, give freely of their understanding of how to walk in deep faith and amazing favor. I have known them for years and never fail to be inspired. When you get a chance to meet them in person, I hope you do it! You'll see what I mean when I say they shine with the anointing of the Lord, with the distinguishing mark of His presence. Their love for people so sincerely opens the door for you to know them, and learn from them.

Enjoy the journey, and live distinguished!

Tracy Swager

Life Coach and Co-Founder

Walking with Swager (*www.walkingwithswager.com*)

FOREWORD

I have known pastors Jeremy and Consuela Roach for many years and can tell you that their lives are a living expression of lives surrendered unto God. I am in awe at how intricately they have patiently knit together the heart, the mind and the word of God in *Living Distinguished*. Their insight breathes such life into "living the gospel." Anchored in sound biblical doctrine, the message opens the hearts and the minds to a deeper, more intimate life available to each of us. The following is a short excerpt from chapter one that gives us a glimpse of the treasures within *"Living Distinguished."*

> *"The heart of God is that you would come to truly know (yada) Him through having an intimate relationship with Him. This is refer-ring to an experiential knowledge of God. It's in this intimate rela-tionship and this secret place with God that we come to know the mind of God, the heart of God, His secrets, and His ways. Moses' request to God was to "show me now Your way, that I may know (yada) You" (Exodus 33:13, NKJV). To truly know him is not to have head knowledge of Him but to allow Him to captivate your heart by His love."*

The clarion call of God's love, His gospel, and His heart unfolds beautifully from chapter to chapter throughout the pages of this book clearly showing us the spiritual process by which the transforming power of grace shapes and forms us into sons and daughters of God. If you are like me and are longing for a more intimate walk with God, I highly recommend *Living Distinguished.* It will not only inspire you to go deeper; it shows you the way.

Enjoy the journey,
Pastor Steven Hall
Rivers of Living Water Church

INTRODUCTION

It should never be hard or a tall task to come up with some words to best describe the life of Jesus. Even those who choose not to believe in His deity and claim as the Son of God would have an intentional choice of words to use when describing what they have read in the Bible. As we take a glance at the days and life of Jesus, none of us would have difficulty describing His life. With the various words that any would use to define the life of our Lord and Savior, I can guarantee that normal, standard, average or mediocre would never be a part of that vocabulary. No one would describe His ministry as typical, ordinary or usual. Instead, the words that would best be used would be extraordinary, exceptional, amazing and remarkable. Never did He blend in with the crowd, He always stood out.

This degree of standing out should be the same for those who personally know Jesus as their Lord and Savior. The question becomes, "Why wouldn't these words ever be used to describe us? Why aren't the people who are close to us, our neighbors, co-workers, family and friends describing our lives in the same manner?" Ask yourself, "What words have been used lately to define who I am and the way I live?"

Normal, average and mediocre should never be used to describe someone who has Jesus living on the inside of them. Jesus did not die for your sins just for you to live a normal life. He came that you *"may have life, and that they may have it more abundantly" (John 10:10, NKJV)*. He redeemed you to live a distinguished life. A life of power, a life of grace and a life of abundance.

The intent of this book is to point us back to the Good News of Jesus and His Kingdom. Not only its relevance in our world today, but how the Kingdom is where we find our purpose and where our significance is defined. As you learn to live distinguished, you will be exposed to all of the substitutes that we have used to produce the results that only the Kingdom can provide. This book will challenge you with the truth and the simplicity of the Gospel. It will charge you to practically change the societies that surround you. I just want you to know that you now have the right to no longer live a normal life, but to live distinguished.

The challenge to living a distinguished life is that it is so much easier to settle for the status quo of life, instead of being used to raise the bar. We have been "okay" fitting into the normalcy and mediocrity of life. When it is God who has called us to stand out, be set apart and live distinguished for Him. It was said of Daniel in the Bible that he *"distinguished himself above the administrators and satraps because he had an extraordinary spirit..." (Daniel 6:3, HCSB).* To be distinguished is to be "marked by eminence, distinction or excellence (Merriam-Webster). It is God's will for each one of His people, those redeemed by His grace, to be set apart, marked by a spirit of excellence and to be known for their extraordinary spirit, character, nature and works.

It is God's heart and desire for you to be equipped to go into the various arenas of society and show the world what Jesus can do with a willing and yielded vessel. *"For the eyes of the Lord run to and fro throughout the whole earth, to show Himself strong on behalf of those whose heart is loyal to Him" (2 Chronicles 16:9, NKJV).* Our lives are to speak volumes of God's nature, character, ability, and goodness. To live a distinguished life for the Lord is to be a part of a people who are advancing God's Kingdom.

Whether the world knows it or not, it needs you to live a distinguished life for God. The world is waiting for someone to show them Heaven's solutions for earth's problems. God's Word is full of answers to our daily dilemmas. Jesus is the answer! He has the answers, and He desires to use us to reveal them to a hurting world. *"These who have turned the world upside down have come here too" (Acts 17:6, NKJV).* It is now time for those who are around us to begin to say the same about us.

"Living Distinguished" will bring clarity of where we fit into God's plan to influence and change the societies that surround us. It's designed to help bring clarity and answers to the questions of why am I here? How will God use me for His Glory? What is my purpose and what makes me different in life? To discover the answers to these questions is the beginning of learning to live distinguished.

There is a clarion call for someone to stand up and be willing to stand out for Christ. There is a call for a generation that will be willing to reveal the true nature and character of God. There is a call for a culture of people to be known for their answers and not their problems. Will you be the one who is willing to answer that call? As you answer His call, you will learn to live a distinguished life for God's glory. If you are willing to answer this call, your life will never be the same. On your mark, get set, and let's go!

A joy to work w/ Express your feeling
Very well outstanding person

beautiful person inside & out, she is always
positive flow of energy

Nice person good coworker

1

Distinguished By His Presence

If there was one thing that was responsible for setting you apart, distinguishing you and defining your significance in life, what would it be? Would it be the eloquent words that you proclaim in prayer? Would it be the size of your Bible or your knowledge of it? Perhaps it would be the people that you know. Or your family name or maybe the education that you have acquired.

As great as all of these things may be, you may be shocked to know that none of these things in themselves distinguishes you. None of them will set you apart to accomplish God's plans for your life. I have come to believe that the answer to this question is found in the writing of Moses. *"How will anyone know that you look favorably on me—on me and on your people—if you don't go with us? For your presence among us sets your people and me apart from all other people on the earth"* *(Exodus 33:16, NLT).*

Moses comes to realize that what would distinguish God's people from other's on earth was God Himself. As God's presence was with them, they would find favor, (Exodus 33:13) safety and peace (Exodus 33:14) and learn to live distinguished. It was, and still is, by God's presence, that we are to be known. God's desire has always been that His people would carry His presence into every atmosphere, even to the degree that others would notice a difference when around us.

When we come to realize that it is God's presence that defines our significance, we can go onto our jobs and serve as a constant hope of encouragement. It is His presence that will be attributed to us getting results in all that we would do. Your next promotion may come simply as a result of God's hand on your life. Productivity and progression would be our expectation every day of our lives.

We would be able to see things that surround us differently. We would be better positioned to bring solutions to the problems that are around us. In His presence, we are empowered to live a victorious life for the Kingdom of God. It is in His presence that we come to know who God is and who we are in God.

Everything Else

Instead of acknowledging that it is God Himself who defines our significance in life, we often use everything else. It is only then that we realize that there are no other substitutes for God. How does this happen? It is the result of our willingness to put everything else before and in place of God.

In my life, I have personally attempted to use various things to make me feel important before others. I have used clothes and wardrobes to make me appear significant. I have used connections and people that I knew to make me feel distinguished. I have used money to make me feel superior. I have even tried to use my knowledge and experience in life to make me look important before others. Truth be told, all of us have done so and perhaps in many ways, we still try to use everything but God to set us apart for greatness.

The temptation to define our significance by our abilities is evident throughout our society. It's seen in the basketball player whose identity and value has always been wrapped up in his ability to play amongst the elite in this world. He will still attempt to play beyond his time just because basketball has been the only thing that has brought value to his life. It's seen in the Hollywood actress whose career on the big screen has brought her to the highest of heights in all of entertainment. Whenever someone more beautiful, creative and entertaining appears on the scene, she doesn't know how to go about life because her identity has been wrapped in the applause of others.

It is imperative that we realize that it is not what we have that defines our identities in life. It is who we have and who we are in Christ that distinguishes us. It is not our ability that defines the legacy that we will leave with others. It's His power and grace at work in our lives by which we are to be remembered. Without truly knowing who God is, we always look for the external things of life to fill the internal void; a void which can only be filled by God.

Favor In His Presence

The favor of God was experienced among the Israelites when God's presence traveled with them. In fact, Moses and God's people did not have to wait to get to the promise land to experience God's goodness. While in the wilderness, they experienced God's favor simply because God was with them. The same is true with Joseph. In Genesis 37, the Bible mentions how Joseph was given a "coat of many colors" by his beloved father, and that his brothers *"hated him and could not speak peaceably to him" (Genesis 37:4, NKJV).*

If you were to read this story too fast, you would be left to believe that it was his coat that brought so much favor into Joseph's life. Once again it would be easy to think that it is the accumulation of wealth, fame, ability and materials that would produce favor in the sight of others. All of us have a "coat of many colors" that we believe is what defines our significance in life. There is a uniqueness in all of our lives that we have been using to distinguish us from everyone else. In many cases, if we were to lose "our coat of many colors" we would lose our sense of identity as well.

I would like to suggest that it wasn't Joseph's fancy coat that gave him favor or made him significant. Rather, it was the fact that his God was with him at all times. After being thrown into a ditch, sold into slavery and bought by Potiphar, the Bible still records that God was with him. *"The Lord was with Joseph, and he was a successful man; and he was in the house of his master the Egyptian" (Genesis 39:2, NKJV).*

What an amazing statement! It didn't say that the coat was with Joseph, and he was successful. It didn't even say that his father Israel was with him, and he was successful. It says that God was with Joseph, and he became successful and favored by God. God's blessing was upon him as he served Potiphar.

Joseph's success and favor wasn't contingent on his surroundings or season. Often we have been taught to believe that God's favor seems to be contingent on a timing and a season. Many have been left to believe that they have to wait for their surroundings to change before they can walk into God's goodness. Or that their circumstances have to change before they can experience God's favor. God's word has to become more of a reality than your circumstances, and our favor with God is never determined by a season. Instead, your season shall always be determined by the favor that you already have with God.

> *"And his master (Potiphar) saw that the Lord was with him (Joseph) and that the Lord made all he did to prosper in his hand. So Joseph found favor in his sight and served him" (Genesis 39:3-4, NKJV).*

Joseph was in a miserable season of slavery. Nothing is favorable about slavery. The good news was that he wasn't by himself. The presence that was with Joseph is what made the difference. Later on in Joseph's story, he would be sent to prison, yet still found favor. And even in prison, *"the Lord was with Joseph and showed him mercy, and He gave him favor" (Genesis 39:21, NKJV).* Even when he had made it out of prison and was placed before Pharaoh, Joseph would still find favor. It was Pharaoh who would ask, *"Can we find such a one as this, a man in whom is the Spirit of God?" (Genesis 41:38, NKJV).*

Do you want to know how to find favor in the sight of others? Learn that favor is first found in God's presence. Your favor is defined by a relationship with Jesus and learning to rest in His presence. It was the very presence of God that set Joseph apart and distinguished him.

If we were to skip over into the New Testament, there is a story of Peter and John being apprehended and questioned by the leaders of the law. *"Now when they saw the boldness of Peter and John and perceived that they were uneducated and untrained men, they marveled. And they realized that they had been with Jesus" (Acts 4:13, NKJV).* Despite the education, training or the lack thereof, and the fact that everyone knew that Peter and John were "ordinary fishermen," these followers of Jesus were able to operate in boldness, power, miracles, and authority.

The people who saw this "marveled" at them and they knew that these men had "been with Jesus." Being with Jesus is what makes the difference in everything that we do. Being with Jesus is what will lead us to live a distinguished life. As a believer in Christ, there should be some aspect of our lives that lets others know that we "have been with Jesus."

People on our jobs should "marvel" at our consistency to show up and our character to serve. In our communities, people should "marvel" at how our lives have become a witness to the grace of God. Those who are sick among us should "marvel" as God's healing power becomes present among us. All of this simply because God's presence is with us.

In today's society, people have become defined by their education and knowledge. Even if you may lack an education, connections, or a good credit score, as long as you have a relationship with God, you will always have more than enough. You can say as Peter did: *"Silver and gold I do not have, but what I do have I give you: In the name of Jesus Christ of Nazareth, rise up and walk" (Acts 3:6, NKJV)*. Once again, it's not what you have that shall distinguish you. It's who you have that makes all of the difference. Favor is found in the very presence of our God.

Manifested Presence

So you may ask, what is the presence of God? Great question. When I reference the presence of God I am referring to the manifestation of His tangible presence, and power within the lives of His people. I know that you must be asking yourselves, "Well isn't God all around us? Doesn't His presence rest among all of His creation?" Yes, you would be right; our God is "Omnipresent." To be Omnipresent is to be "present in all places and at all times" (Merriam-Webster). There has never been, and there will never be a time in which God Himself would not be present everywhere and at the same time.

> *"Can anyone hide himself in secret places, So I shall not see him?" says the Lord; "Do I not fill heaven and earth?" says the Lord" (Jeremiah 23:24, NKJV). "I can never escape from your Spirit! I can never get away from your presence! If I go up to heaven, you are there; if I go down to the grave, you are there. If I ride the wings of the morning, if I dwell by the farthest oceans, even there your hand will guide me, and your strength will support me." (Psalm 139:7-10, NLT).*

God is the only one who has this ability. As awesome as the knowledge of the Omnipresence of God is, what brings about transformation is the manifestation of God's presence within our lives. The manifestation of His presence is when His omnipresence becomes tangible. It is when the invisible presence of God becomes visible and evident to display His miracles and wonders. It is when God Himself demonstrates His glory in our surroundings and circumstances.

As you pursue more of God in your life, you will soon realize that there is nothing greater than experiencing the fullness of His presence. *"In Your presence is fullness of joy; At Your right hand are pleasures forevermore" (Psalms 16:11, NKJV).* The greatest privilege that a believer has in this lifetime is the fact that God has decided to have His Holy presence to dwell among us, and within us. Learning to live distinguished isn't about living a self-centered life with our focus being on what God can do for us. Rather, it is being God-centered and allowing Him to live His life in us. A distinguished life is one in which one's affections and focus are centered on the presence of God. It is His presence that prepares us for a life of greatness.

The Greenhouse of God

There are libraries and bookstores that are filled with self-help books designed to assist you in developing greatness. There is a plethora of conferences and motivational speakers from all over the world that specialize in motivating you to maximize your potential. Certainly, there are no shortages of inspirational messages that promise a fulfilled prosperous life. Even with all of these inspirational messages for success, none of them can measure up to the significance of a relationship with God.

I am fully persuaded that greatness is defined and developed in the presence of God. In fact, I believe that greatness and success are nothing but a result of His presence. Apart from God, everything else falls short. *"But I am like an olive tree, thriving in the house of God. I will always trust in God's unfailing love" (Psalms 52:8, NLT).*

David says that we are like the olive tree which in the right climate is a beautiful and fruitful tree, and we are to thrive in the house of God. Yes, in God's presence we are to thrive, prosper, flourish and succeed. We are to live distinguished as we rest in Him. If we are to be an olive tree that is to thrive and flourish, then it is His manifested presence that serves as the greenhouse in which we are to dwell.

Typically, greenhouses serve the purpose of protecting various plants and vegetation from the excess of cold and hot weather. They also protect from the dangerous pests that could cause harm to the growth of the plants. The same is true with a relationship with Jesus and God's presence. In the greenhouse of God, we are planted in Him. We are thriving because of Him, and learning to live a distinguished life for Him.

Regardless of the outside dangers, harmful environments or disastrous circumstances, this greenhouse shall protect us from them all. The greenhouse of God will empower us to succeed. God's presence shall provide everything that we would need in this life to prosper. God's presence is the incubator for greatness. You can say that everything that we would need is in a relationship with God.

What the phone booth was to Clark Kent, known as Superman, is what God's presence is to a believer in Christ. It was in this booth that an ordinary man became Superman. It is also in a relationship with Jesus that we too have become a "new creation." It was in the phone booth that transformation took place, and he was able to save the world.

As we rest in God's presence, we are transformed and able to help bring salvation to the world. What's greater than Clark Kent's phone booth is that God's presence isn't stationary. Instead, He is mobile, and He desires for us to take Him everywhere that we go. God desires to use His people to become carriers of His presence.

Being a Carrier

> "Now when they drew near Jerusalem, and came to Bethphage, at the Mount of Olives, then Jesus sent two disciples, saying to them, "Go into the village opposite you, and immediately you will find a donkey tied and a colt with her. Loose them and bring them to Me. And if anyone says anything to you, you shall say, 'The Lord has need of them,' and immediately he will send them." All this was done that it might be fulfilled which was spoken by the prophet, saying: "Tell the daughter of Zion, 'Behold, your King is coming to you, Lowly, and sitting on a donkey, a colt, the foal of a donkey." (Matthew 21:1-5, NKJV).

This story is right before Jesus was to complete His final assignment as He would go to the Cross. In this passage, Jesus commissions His disciples to find and loosen a donkey and colt that had been tied up, for Jesus had need of them. The purpose for this donkey and the colt was to carry the presence of Jesus wherever

He desired to go so that Jesus could be celebrated before the people. What if our purpose and assignment in life were to simply carry the presence of God?

Not wherever we wanted to go, but wherever He wants us to go? What if our significance on earth was to carry His presence before others so that they may glorify our God? Perhaps the significance of our existence is that we are to be the carriers of His Glory? What if people were to recognize that God was with us and was to desire to become carriers of God as well?

Let's say that you were to ask, "What does it mean to carry the presence of God?" "How do I become a carrier of God's presence?" To be a carrier of His presence is to be one who centers his/her entire life, focus and affection on God and His glory. As I spend time with God, I will become more attuned to who He is and with His tangible presence with me at all times.

> *"I am with you always, even to the end of the age" (Matthew 28:20, NASB). "For the LORD your God goes with you; he will never leave you nor forsake you." (Deuteronomy 31:6, NKJV).*

What awesome promises! What's even greater than these promises is the fact that the Creator of the universe likes to hang out with us. Through His Son, God has promised that His presence will never leave us. In essence, you can never carry something that you haven't been immersed in for yourself. It's when you have spent quiet time with the Lord and isolated yourself from everything else, that you will begin to experience the manifestation of His presence. This all begins with what Jesus references as the secret place

The Secret Place

> *"But you, when you pray, go into your inner room, close your door and pray to your Father who is in secret, and your Father who sees what is done in secret will reward you openly" (Matthew 6:6, NASB).*

The secret place is the quiet place in your life in which only you and God meet. It is the starting line to experiencing a distinguished life. The secret place can be your bedroom, closet, couch or even your shower. The location is not significant. What is important is that it's a place where you are willing to seek God and become vulnerable in His presence. It's in this secret place with the Father that He begins to reveal His plans for the day, His strategies for that season and His heart for His children.

> *"Be still, and know that I am God; I will be exalted among the nations, I will be exalted in the earth" (Psalms 46:10, NKJV).*

The command in this passage is to "Be still." Where is the best place to "be still?" In God's presence, in the secret place with the Lord. What is amazing about this passage is that the command to "Be Still" is followed up by "and know that I am God."

The word "know" in Hebrew is the word "yada." Which is used for the word "knew" when the Bible says that, *"Now Adam knew Eve his wife, and she conceived" (Genesis 4:1, NKJV).* This Hebrew word carries various meanings, one which means to know through intimacy. I would like to suggest that it is not enough to just have head knowledge about God. Or knowledge about the various doctrines of Christianity.

The heart of God is that you would come to truly know (yada) Him through having an intimate relationship with Him. This is referring to an experiential knowledge of God. It's in this intimate relationship and this secret place with God that we come to know the mind of God, the heart of God, and His secrets. Moses' request to God was to *"show me now Your way, that I may know (yada) You" (Exodus 33:13, NKJV).* To truly know Him is not to have head knowledge of Him, but to allow Him to captivate your heart by His love. It is in this secret place that we will come to truly know Him and learn to live a distinguished life.

I know that you may be saying, "Well I'm always busy, and I'm not sure if I have the time to carve out for this secret place." Or maybe your thoughts are, "I'm not too comfortable just sitting still in silence." Both of these thoughts are normal to have while in pursuit of developing a relationship with God. As you make God your top priority in all that you do, while in the midst of your day, you will begin to crave these quiet times in the secret place with the Lord.

In fact, you'll soon realize that God was never concerned with your finding time for Him, but rather your willingness to make time for Him. God will begin to lead you in the amount and the measure of time that He desires for you to still away with Him. I have come to find out personally that it isn't always the amount of time that is important. It is the quality of that time that is spent resting in God's presence.

When our son Landon Jeremyah was born, I would intentionally sit at his bedside waiting for him to wake up. I would anticipate spending time with him. I would watch him move around. I'd see his eyes begin to blink hoping that they would remain open. Landon couldn't give me the amount of time that I desired for us to have spent together. Whatever time he was able to give me I would have made the most out of it.

It was in that season that God spoke to me. Just as I would wait at Landon's bedside for him to spend time with me, so did God also wait by my side just for me to acknowledge His presence and spend time with Him. I would have loved to have spent hours at a time with Landon, but I was willing to take whatever time that he would give me, even if it were only ten minutes. The same is true with God and His people.

Holding Landon in my arms, I realized that it was not what he could offer me in the relationship, but it was all about my love for him. The only way that my son could have learned to love me was by me first loving him. Landon could only come to know of his father's love by spending time with me. So it is true that we too come to know the love of our Heavenly Father by spending time with Him in the secret place.

For God's people to overcome the problem of having to sit still, the fear of silence must be addressed. I believe that the fear of silence has become an epidemic in our society. Everywhere we go there is noise, commotion and activity taking place.

At times I am challenged to deal with the need to always have something going on around me. Whether it is the television remaining on while sleeping, music on throughout the day or talking on my phone while driving. There is rarely a time where silence is prevalent throughout my day.

Even within our churches, we have equated noise with Godly activity or the move of God. It is when the minister is encouraging the people to praise the Lord that we reference the move of God. Somewhat implying that it's our noise that moves God. Or that God only decides to move when there is noise.

There is a story of a gentleman who had asked a certain lady to attend one of his church services. To his surprise, she gladly accepted. The people of God were in a high praise during this enthusiastic service. Afterward, the gentlemen asked his friend what she thought of the service. Her reply was, "Everything was great, the atmosphere was electric, and the presence of God was there." The gentleman was greatly pleased that she had enjoyed herself. It was her next question that caught the gentleman off guard. In the sincerest way, she asked him, "but at what part of the service does the church sit still in silence to hear what God has to say?"

It was the prophet Elijah who was positioned to experience the move of God by way of a "great and strong wind." It was clear that God wasn't in the wind. After the wind, there was an earthquake, but God wasn't in the earthquake. Then there was a fire, but God wasn't in the fire. Elijah did not experience God in any of these events, but God decided to reveal Himself in a *"still small voice" (1 Kings 19:12, NKJV)*. It is of equal importance that we remain mindful that many of our experiences are to be within the quiet times as we rest, sit still and yield in His presence.

It can be uncomfortable for most people to remain silent in the same room with someone that they do not know. It is normal for all of us to begin to develop the need to break the silence and start a conversation, crack a joke or introduce ourselves. Many of us are only comfortable sitting still and being silent around those that we know. The same can be true with God. We should not live with the notion that every time we come to the secret place with God we are to do all of the talking. Perhaps God has something that He wants to say, and I can guarantee that whatever He says can be a life changing impact.

Remaining Conscious of His Presence

What happens when you have to leave this secret place, this quiet time with God? Can we still experience His presence while at work, in the grocery store, chatting with our neighbors and so forth? Perhaps these are questions that you have asked yourself. The good news is that His presence isn't stationary; it is mobile. The manifested presence of God can be experienced everywhere you go. It should not come as a surprise that God's tangible presence is within us and upon us as He has now made His throne upon the hearts of His people. From Genesis to Revelation there are countless examples and promises of God dwelling among His people. Knowing that God is forever with me is no longer contingent on a feeling but now by my conviction of His word. His name is Emmanuel, which means *"God is with us" (Matthew 1:23, NLT)*.

Another way to remain mindful of God's presence is to develop the ability to discern His move and His presence. God desires us to discern and learn to recognize His presence and movements so that we can move with Him in the earth. This level of discernment isn't to be developed in a seminary or divinity school alone but is best established during those quiet times with Jesus. In other words, if you want to be one who is used by God in public before others, you must be one who has first spent time with God in private. It is in an intimate relationship with Jesus that we will begin to distinguish His presence, heart, move, and will.

The last point that I will expound on when learning to remain conscious of His presence is the importance of thinking about His goodness at all times. I have come to learn that the presence of God being revealed and manifested can be only one thought away. There have been so many times that my wife and I would begin to talk about the goodness of God. Just to realize that the very presence of God had manifested.

When you have experienced His grace and blessings, it should never become hard to begin to think about what all He has done. It is during these moments that it seems like God sees someone reverencing Him, or He hears of someone speaking well of Him, and He decides to show up. *"Then those who feared the Lord spoke to one another, and the Lord listened and heard them; So a book of remembrance was written before Him for those who fear the Lord and who meditate on His name"* (Malachi 3:16, NKJV).

God desires for us to be a people who are used to help usher in His presence into every environment. It's at the grocery store with the lady who is immobile that He desires you to remain conscious of His presence and carry His power so that she may experience His healing grace. She may have come in for some food, but she left with God's healing. It's in the public school where there are daily threats of violence, chaos, and disorder. As you are preparing to teach the students about mathematics, the Lord is preparing to teach others how to follow Him as He uses your life to do so.

Too many believers have been like Jacob when it comes to God's presence. *"Surely the Lord is in this place, and I did not know it"* (Genesis 28:16, NKJV). This should not be our testimony. Let's be a people who have learned to discern the move of His presence and become distinguished by His glory. Let's be a people who have been set apart by His manifestation and let His existence in us define our significance in life.

2

Distinguished By The Gospel

Alady called me for prayer for her marriage as she was excited in having been a newlywed for only one day. She was asking that God would bless and protect her husband and her daughter. Before prayer, I asked her, "What is your current relationship with Jesus?" She responds, "I believe in God but I am not a Christian. I attend church every week, and I am a faithful member of the church, but I haven't accepted Jesus as my Lord and Savior yet."

I chose to keep listening and not bombard her with a plethora of scriptures. She explained that she had been in an abusive relationship with the father of her daughter. She had now begun a new relationship with a better guy. At this point, the Holy Spirit is nudging me to present the Gospel to her.

It would be God who would help bring her to a place where she would see the need for Jesus. I explained to her that just as she was in a relationship that was harmful to her life and the life of her daughter, so were we all by living in the fallen nature of sin. God sent His Son to die for her sins. I reminded her of how she was able to get away from the old abusive relationship and was able to begin a better one. This new relationship is also the case with Jesus. It is through Jesus that He has made a way for us to be removed from an old abusive life of sin to be restored back to a fruitful relationship with our loving Father.

If He was good enough to bring her into a new relationship with her husband without knowing Jesus, how much more would she see God's goodness while in a relationship with Jesus? At this point, I explained that it wouldn't be the repeating of my prayer that would bring her into salvation. It would be the fact that she would believe with her heart and confess with her mouth that Jesus is the Son of God and that He died for her sins. It was at this point that the God that she had only heard about became her Savior. She accepted His Gospel and began a new relationship with Him.

As exhilarating as this moment was, she ended our conversation with an alarming statement. "I have never heard this message of God's good news explained like this before. I feel like I can now praise God in a greater way." (She was actively a participant in the church's choir). Wow, that threw me for a loop!

I was amazed at the thought of someone faithfully worshipping in the choir but had never heard the Gospel. How many more are like my sister? Singing but they have not given their heart to the one they are singing about; Jesus. There are many who are faithful members of the church and have even served in church, yet still, haven't heard the true Gospel. Repeating a prayer, being baptized out of religious routine, but yet fail to have heard the only true message that has the power to bring salvation.

Our church attendance does not earn us our salvation in the Lord. It is imperative that God's people return to the truth and the death, burial, and resurrection of Jesus. A distinguished life begins with our ability to receive the authentic message that God poured out His wrath on Jesus for our sins. There is only one message that can restore us back to our original position in God's family. That message is the true unadulterated Gospel of Jesus Christ.

Different Answers

If you were to ask ten people the one question of why Jesus came to earth, I would imagine that there would be the potential for ten different answers. They would probably range from, "He came to provide us an example of how to live life," to "He came to do miracles and display His awesome and great power." Perhaps some would say that Jesus came "as a prophet to bring hope to humanity." I've even heard some people say, "I believe that Jesus was real and that He did come to earth, but He is not the only way to Heaven."

There would be many different responses to this one question. If I were to ask Jesus why He was sent to earth, I'd imagine that He would respond to us by saying, *"The thief does not come except to steal, and to kill, and to destroy. I have come that they may have life and that they may have it more abundantly" (John 10:10, NKJV).* Jesus would reference the fact He was sent to earth to restore all of humanity back into a right relationship with God. He came to restore us back to our original identities as children of God. This is the result of Jesus' death, burial, and resurrection. This is what the Apostle Paul called the Gospel, in which he was not ashamed, for *"it is the power of God unto salvation."*

The good news of Jesus should become practical and impact every area of our lives. What the world needs is some good news, some hope, and inspiration. What the world needs to know is that God became as a man, lived on earth, never sinned and took all of this life's calamities to the Cross. What this world needs is someone who knows of this Gospel, has been distinguished by this Gospel and can live out this good news before others.

What is the Gospel?

The word Gospel means "good news" or "to bring or announce good news." The Gospel is to have a message of victory with the intent of sharing and announcing this good news to others. It is to have a message that would bring gladness and joy to those who are to hear it. It is best illustrated in the messenger who has been sent back to his nation or homeland to announce the victory that has been won through battle. So it is true with us. Just as humanity has had many battles and casualties, there is good news that we now have access to victory over the issues of life through Jesus.

For the one who has battled cancer, in Christ, there is good news of healing. It is "by His stripes we are healed." For the one who has battled unemployment, there's good news in Jesus. Doors are opened, and we now have a purpose in Christ. For the brother who has been wearied by the battle of not knowing his identity, the good news of Jesus is that he has been "made in God's image." For the sister who has battled poverty all of her life, in Christ, she has now been made wealthy by God's grace. No matter what your battle, fight or war has been, there is good news for you!

Many of this world's religions teach on the fact that you will have to seek and pursue their god to be forgiven of your sins. The Gospel of Jesus is the only teaching that makes the claim that God sought after and pursued us. The Son of God died in our place, and we are now forgiven through Jesus. In every other religion, it is all about how much they are to demonstrate their love for their god. While our teachings are all about God demonstrating His love for us.

"While we were still sinners, Christ died for us" (Romans 5:8, NKJV). The fact that Jesus died for us is how we know that God loves us. God didn't wait for you to get yourself together to send His Son. While we were sinning, running from Him and wanted nothing to do with Him, Jesus still died in our place and took on our punishments. Now that is good news!

Here and Now

What's not good news, is if we had to wait until we get to Heaven to enjoy salvation. The Gospel is news worth rejoicing over knowing that our soul will find its eternal rest in the Lord. One day we will all get to see Jesus face to face. This is good news! What is also good news is that as believers in Jesus we have the privilege of experiencing a bit of Heaven here and now.

When we hear people teach on having salvation in Jesus, it is usually taught on having an "eternal life." However, salvation isn't just the concept of having an eternal life, but it is also referencing that in God we now have access to a quality of life. In the Greek, there is a word called "Zoe" which speaks to having an abundance of life, God kind of life or a life that can only come from God. This kind of life only comes through a relationship with Jesus, and it is to be experienced in this lifetime as well.

God put our worst on His Son Jesus as He went to the Cross so that we could have His very best here and now. The good news of Jesus is that He took the misery of our lives to the Cross so that we may have the abundance of His life. Our Lord and Savior did not take a brutal beating and die a gruesome death just for us to live a miserable life. One may ask, "with all of this wickedness, crime, poverty, and the wars in this world, why don't we ever see this abundance of life?" The condition of this world is the result of the fallen nature of man and the lack of the true Gospel being preached, lived and demonstrated.

It was when the first man (Adam and Eve) disobeyed God and His command to not eat of the forbidden fruit *(Genesis 3:6)* that sin was introduced into the world. Believe it or not, the current conditions and circumstances of this fallen world have been and is the result of sin. Sickness, poverty, war, calamities, depression, confusion and greed are all a result of sin entering into the world. *"And I will put enmity Between you and the woman, and between your seed and her Seed; He shall bruise your head, And you shall bruise His heel" (Genesis 3:15, NKJV).* This promise to bruise the head of the enemy who had enticed Adam and Eve into this sin was fulfilled through Jesus. God had decided to come to earth as a man, live as a man and died for the sins of man. This incarnation was necessary to restore man back to his rightful place in God's family.

> *"Adam's one sin brings condemnation for everyone, but Christ's one act of righteousness brings a right relationship with God and new life for everyone. Because one person disobeyed God, many became sinners. But because one other person obeyed God, many will be made righteous" (Romans 5:18-19, NLT).*

The world is in the state that it's currently in because of the acts of Adam. It will only get worse without the Gospel of Jesus truly being preached to all of the nations. Through Jesus' one act on the Cross, humanity now has access to how life was supposed to be before Adam and Eve sinned in the garden. A life of blessings, fulfillment, peace and abundance while walking with God.

The Gospel is the antidote and cure for the ailments of this world and this life. Every other message, strategy, self-help book and religion is just a diluted substitute. A doctor would never treat a patient that has a virus with a cough suppressant. A wise doctor would only use an antibiotic that will fight off and kill the patient's virus.

The same is true with sin and sickness. The Gospel is the only antidote and cure that has the power to totally eradicate sin and its effects in this world. Jesus died to redeem us from the struggles of sin, sickness and the issues of this world. I just want to encourage you that whatever you have or may be dealing with, He finished it on the Cross.

Cheap Substitutes

Without the Gospel, those who do not personally know God have to resort to finding other substitutes to experience salvation. Without the Gospel being proclaimed and lived out before others, the world will remain in the dark about the truth of Jesus. What we see today is the world's best attempt to fulfill and accomplish only what God can do. Those who have not given their lives to Jesus are left with using everything else in life to bring a sense of purpose.

We have made money, fame, notoriety, acceptance, assets and our accomplishments our idols. These idols have rested upon the thrones that rightfully belong to God, our hearts. Things that we have desired externally have now become an internal longing. We have used houses, cars, money, sex and clothes as a cheap substitute for the Gospel.

There is no sense of salvation, purpose, and fulfillment in these things. I have seen so many people burn themselves out striving for the latest and greatest of things just to remain relevant with the times. There have been many entertainers who have tried to find solace and satisfaction in their careers. It has become sad to see them compromise, sell themselves and settle for less to feel significant.

There are no shortages of reality shows with people who are striving to make a comeback and feel important within today's society. I've heard interviews with rappers who have the cars, women/men, houses and more money than they could have ever imagined. Just to say that they cannot live peacefully in their own homes. To have a good night's sleep is foreign to them. The need to feel successful and significant has had many people to grow tired, weary, and without hope. Whenever they achieve what they were striving for they quickly realize the false hope and fulfillment in their achievements.

One of the clichés of this world has been that "good things happen to good people." Surely, this has not been the case. Many people have believed that if they are good enough and do good for others, this same good will finds its way back to them. Or that their goodness in this lifetime will earn them a way to Heaven.

It's the good people that get in is what many people in the world have taught themselves to believe. No matter how good we may try to be, our best efforts will still fall short of God's standards. Our best efforts in this lifetime will still not earn us a ticket to Heaven. For it is not good people who are accepted by God. It is forgiven and redeemed people who have placed their trust in Jesus.

In watching the world trying to find salvation, many people's lives are like the Israelite's journey in the wilderness. Just going around the same mountain for years and getting nowhere. There is good news for those who have found themselves with an empty void within their lives. The good news is that in Jesus they now have access to a new life.

For those whose lives have been nothing but traveling around the same mountains, there is hope found in Jesus. He is the pathway to a promised land. My prayer for us all is that we will come into the knowledge that all we can strive for in life has already been accomplished in Jesus. All that we will ever need in life is found in Him. *Seek ye first, the Kingdom of God & all these things will be added...*

A Relevant Message

There are many people in the world who would say that Jesus and the church no longer have any relevance in today's time. All that many people relegate the message of Jesus to be is the Ten Commandments. His message and rules no longer have an importance in today's society. The ways of God have become antiquated and obsolete in the eyes of many people.

I can understand why the people who do not know Jesus would believe this. For those of us who do know Jesus, we have not always done the best job demonstrating the Gospel before others. In fact, the message that we have often presented was not good news at all. Just a list of rules and regulations that we have not been able to keep.

Many of God's people are not convinced that the Gospel of Jesus has a relevant place in the world today. Therefore, we have decided to water down, alter and just quite frankly preach a whole other message other than the Gospel. In order to remain relevant, many churches have attempted to add or subtract from the Gospel so that they may gain the ears of hurting and lost people. This is very dangerous. It was the Apostle Paul who said that there was to be a curse on anyone who would preach any other message *(Galatians 1:8-9)*. I am persuaded that the Gospel of Jesus is not only a relevant message all by itself, but that it also has the solutions for all of this world's problems.

Once we have encountered God and His goodness for ourselves, we will have no problem practically explaining and witnessing the Gospel to others. The problem comes when the Gospel is no more than just head knowledge that we have learned from a classroom or a book. It's at these moments that we will often have difficulties understanding and explaining the relevancy of this good news. This good news doesn't need additives or anything else to make it impactful and relevant.

The potency of the Gospel can be compared to the potency of black coffee. Coffee is at its most potent point when it is still just black. It's when the coffee drinker begins to add cream or sugar that they will begin to change the chemical make-up of the coffee and dilute what makes it potent. Not that the coffee won't give the drinker the boost that they may need, but the more that you begin to add additional things to the coffee the more you are likely to weaken its impact. It's when the coffee drinker is willing to substitute the impact of the coffee in exchange for adding some flavor and making it more tasteful, that its potency has been compromised.

The same is true with the Gospel. The Gospel is at its most powerful and potent stage when it is lived and presented straight forward. In fact, if you were to add or take away anything from the Gospel, it is no longer the Gospel at all. We take the risk of giving the people who need it the most a watered down Gospel which doesn't bring about transformation. The best thing that we as God's people can do is to learn what the pure, true and unadulterated Gospel is and present it as it is.

The Gospel of Jesus is enough by itself for God to bring about the conversion that is needed within our lives. When we come into the true knowledge of the Gospel, we will no longer have to have Jesus and some additional philosophies. We will realize that Jesus is more than enough. Not only does Jesus have the answers to all of the issues of this world, but He is the answer to all of the issues of this world.

> *"Him we preach, warning every man and teaching every man in all wisdom, that we may present every man perfect in Christ Jesus"*
> *(Colossians 1:28, NKJV).*

Paul tells us that it is "Him we are to preach." Him and Him alone! There is not a circumstance that the Bible hasn't already addressed and provided the solutions to. There isn't a situation that the Cross of Jesus and His resurrection hasn't already resolved. *"For Christ did not send me to baptize, but to preach the gospel, not with wisdom of words, lest the cross of Christ should be made of no effect"* (1 Corinthians 1:17, NKJV). The Gospel doesn't need our eloquent speech, clever words, fancy illustrations or oratory skills to be effective. The Gospel by itself is more than able to get the job done!

Receive It First

This is usually how it works. You come to Christ, giving your life to the Lord. Then you are to be baptized in the water. Next, you are to come to a Sunday school class which is designed to teach you how to be a Christian. There is absolutely nothing wrong with this process, especially when it is genuine before the Lord.

Once you arrive at the class, the teacher's job is to teach you the guidelines of what you must do to follow Jesus. You must first make it a habit of reading the Bible, pray daily, love others, come to church and last but not least, pay your tithes and offering. Does this sound familiar to you? I'd imagine that it does. Consequently, I have witnessed that it is a process like this that has created people to become religious and condemned when they are not able to do all of these things and keep all of the rules.

I have been guilty of this as I was one of the students that attempted to work myself into a relationship with Jesus. I was also one of those teachers who spent the first few months teaching new believers what was expected from them as disciples. In essence, my thought process was that God was more concerned about what you could do for Him as opposed to His people first learning what He has already done for us.

Regardless of what age someone may be when they first decide to come to Jesus, at this point, we are all "babes in Christ" and young in our faith. Just like a baby, there's nothing that we can initially do for God that can please Him except believe in Him. It is imperative that we first have the ability to receive what He has already done.

Think about it. While a baby is still in the womb, there is nothing that this child could do for its mother and father. The baby's only job at this point is to stay connected to its mother and receive all of the necessary nutrients that are needed for the baby to grow. The same is true with God and His children. It was God who took the first step to redeeming us, and it is also God who takes the first step in developing a relationship with us.

Initially, God is not concerned with what we can do for Him. The desire of God's heart is for His children to just simply receive Him. His desire is also for us to receive who we are in Him and to acknowledge all that we have as joint heirs with Jesus. So that we may live a life of purpose, it is essential that we come to know all that we have in Jesus.

Our Benefits Package

When someone first starts a job, it is normal for the supervisor or the Human Resources team to first go over their benefits package. These benefits are the perks of joining this company. I remember a time when I had worked for a certain company that provided excellent benefits. Because I was not knowledgeable about my benefits, I paid out of my own pocket the necessary fees to see a physician.

I would soon come to learn a valuable lesson about taking the time to acknowledge what I already had. I would eventually spend money on something that was already covered. I paid the price for not knowing what was in my benefits. It is wise to know what is in your benefits package.

The same is true for being a follower of Jesus. The Gospel of Jesus is our benefits package. Many times, we find ourselves ignorantly trying to become something that He has already made us to be. We find ourselves pursuing things that we already have in God and paying a high price for the things that Jesus has already covered on our behalves. We spend so much time fighting battles that He has already won and praying prayers that He has already answered. Simply because we have failed to know the promises, blessings, and benefits that come with the Gospel.

"Bless the LORD, O my soul, and forget none of His benefits" (Psalms 103:2, NASB). These benefits include salvation, quality of life, peace, provision, purpose, protection and all the promises of God. All of which have already been purchased by Jesus Christ. We have countless promises to healing, and wholeness. God wishes that you *"may prosper in all things and be in health, just as your soul prospers"* (3 John 1:2, NKJV).

When you are in Christ, you are also in covenant with God. To be in covenant means that God has made promises to you that are irrevocable because of Jesus. We are now joint heirs of Jesus' inheritance. In Jesus, we are now beneficiaries of His will, benefactors of His grace and the partakers of His wonderful benefits package. There is nothing that life can throw your way that the "finished works" of Jesus has not already covered. Our benefits package has been loaded with many promises. It is now up to us to know what has been freely given to us within the Gospel, our benefits package.

Freely Given

"Now we have received, not the spirit of the world, but the Spirit, who is from God, that we might know the things that have been freely given to us by God" (1 Corinthians 2:12, NKJV).

I would like to believe that the Spirit of God Himself is our Human Resources Director. He has been assigned to every believer to point us to the promises that we have in the Lord and to help us receive everything that Jesus accomplished through His death. Think about that for a moment. We haven't received the spirit of this world. Instead, we have received God's very own Spirit whose job is to reveal to us what has "been freely given to us by God."

The old cliché that many were brought up on says that "nothing in this world is for free." Implying that whatever you aspire to have or achieve in this world will have a cost. Everything in this lifetime must be earned, whether it's earning it with your time, efforts, energy or money. This mindset is why it is so difficult for God's people to receive something freely from God that we didn't earn. It is so difficult for many believers just to receive God's acceptance without obtaining it through works. Or to just receive God's promises without feeling like they have to qualify for them.

Perhaps you too have felt that if you don't keep God's rules, God will not be pleased with you and that you will miss out on the blessings of God. The good news of Jesus is that your ability to keep God's rules is not what qualifies you for God's blessings. It's the fact that Jesus has fulfilled all of these rules and laws and in Him, you have been freely given all of God's promises.

The Gospel of Jesus is all about the fact that He died for what would have disqualified you. He took what you deserved which was death and gave you what you didn't deserve; His life. If that wasn't enough, He ascended back to Heaven so that His Spirit would dwell within the lives of His followers. The Holy Spirit reveals to us all of the very promises that we now have and the life that we are now to live.

One thing that keeps us from walking into the promises of God is our attempts to work for them. It's at this point that we begin to hinder the very blessings of God from flowing into our lives. Imagine receiving a bonus check from your employer, a free gift from the company. How ridiculous would it sound for someone to clock back in and work before they could receive, cash or deposit this bonus check? That is how many people are today. Instead of just receiving what has been freely given, we feel like we have to clock back in and put in some work before we can just receive and walk into what is rightfully ours in Christ.

Well, you may ask, "what is it that has been freely given?" God's salvation has been freely given. His favor, goodness, and kindness in our lives have been freely given. God's promises for provision and victory has been freely given. God's promises being freely given to you is not contingent on your Bible reading, disciplined prayer life, church attendance, or your obedience to keeps God's law. Instead, all of His promises and blessings are granted to His people simply because of Jesus. My question to you is, "what areas of your life have you been working for God's blessings instead of just receiving what He Has already done for you?"

The fact that Jesus died for your sins so that you may have life must be more of a reality than your circumstances. The Bible tells us that *"the just shall live by his faith" (Habakkuk 2:4, NKJV)*. Our life and existence are to be lived by our faith in Jesus. God's blessings are not obtained by waiting for our circumstances to change, but rather by acknowledging that in Jesus we have victory over every circumstance.

Starting from Victory

When we begin to realize the good news of Jesus for every area of our lives, then we will also begin to realize that in Him we have victory. We are no longer to try to fight and work to obtain victory. In fact, we start off our mornings and our days in victory. Our ability to walk into victory each day will not be based on our performances at work, nor our ability to complete a daily task list. None of these things will ever help to truly define your significance in life. It is when we learn to live with His life and His accomplishments that we will learn to live distinguished.

Imagine an Olympic athlete standing at the podium in all of his splendor and glory accepting his gold medal. He is recognized as the best at what he does. He is honored as the champion. Now imagine Jesus, who went to the Cross on our behalf. Instead of a gold medal, He was given a crown of thorns.

God raised Jesus from the grave. He is now resting in a place of victory, and seated at the right hand of the throne. What is amazing is that we are also seated in this place of victory with Jesus. Where He sits at the right hand of God the Father is a place of honor, authority, favor and victory in life, and we are seated with Him.

So imagine starting off your day conscious of the victory from where you are seated. Imagine going into every business meeting knowing that you are highly favored of the Lord. As you have favor with God Himself, He will give you amazing favor with man. In today's time, having a good name and a reputation before others will help to esteem you as being honorable.

Imagine having His name, which is the name that is above all names and His reputation that shall precede you. It's His name, favor, and honor that shall "open doors for you that no man shall close." It's His authority that He has given unto us that will allow us to speak blessings into every situation. When His hand is on your life, other people will not be able to ignore the favor that surrounds you.

People will recognize that something is different with you and that it has not been the world's ways of obtaining success. It will not be the world's strategies for networking nor the accumulation of the world's wealth that has set you apart. It is simply the fact that you have decided to follow Jesus. It is the fact He has decided to live His life in you.

Our Victory Lap

> *"Let us run with endurance the race that is set before us, looking unto Jesus, the author, and finisher of our faith, who for the joy that was set before Him endured the cross" (Hebrews 12:1-2, NKJV).*

Think about it this way; in the Bible, life is referenced as a race. God gives His people the strategy of how to run this race called life. I love how the New Living Translation puts it into context.

> *"And let us run with endurance the race God has set before us. We do this by keeping our eyes on Jesus, the champion who initiates and perfects our faith. Because of the joy awaiting him, he endured the cross, disregarding its shame. Now he is seated in the place of honor beside God's throne" (Hebrews 12:1-2, NLT).*

So if this life is a race that we are to run, the key to running this life well is to "keep our eyes on Jesus," who is the "champion who initiates and perfects our faith." We are to keep our minds, and our hearts centered on Jesus and what He has accomplished on our behalf. We must remain mindful, that the Gospel is to have the most impact on every area of our lives.

It was Jesus, the Son of God, who showed us how to run this race of life. In all actuality, He ran and completed His race at the Cross. The Cross was His finish line, and it's the very place where our starting line for victory begins. And now He is at the champion's podium, "seated in the place of honor beside God's throne."

The race that we could not run, Jesus ran for us. He completed a sinless and righteous life on our behalf. The great news about His race is that His victory has now become our victory. Depending on how you choose to live this life, your race can feel like a marathon, or it can feel more like a victory lap.

When you choose to try to accomplish a life of significance with your achievements, life will feel like a marathon. I am not saying that life will always be easy, but I am certain that your race will be more like running His victory lap when living from His finished works. Living a distinguished life is living a life that is designed to carry out His victory.

Victory Over Darkness

The good news of Jesus and His victory is also seen and demonstrated over the powers of darkness. It is imperative that we are cognizant that there is an enemy that does exist. His primary job has been to keep people from coming into the knowledge of the Gospel of Jesus. In fact, much of the resistance you experience when walking with Jesus has been at the hands of the enemy. Many of the thoughts of suicide, depression, fear, and low self-esteem have been because of the demonic activity in the lives of many.

"The thief does not come except to steal, and to kill, and to destroy" (John 10:10, NKJV). This thief, referenced as the "devil", "Satan", "accuser of the brethren" or even the "father of lies", was originally known by the name of "Lucifer" *(Isaiah 14:12).* This thief has taken advantage of the fallen state of man. He has also used those who were once created in God's image to push his agenda into the earth.

The enemy has a team of fallen angels who exist to carry out his plans over territories, nations, and even the minds and lives of individual people. The enemy does have influence and power, but the good news is that his power has been nullified from the lives of God's people. They have been redeemed, set free, empowered and given authority to enforce the victory of Jesus over the forces of darkness.

As a believer in Christ, we are to be seated, rested and positioned into a place of authority and victory over Satan. *"The Son of God was manifested, that He might destroy the works of the devil"* (1 John 3:8, NKJV). Jesus destroyed the works and the plans that Satan had for humanity. Jesus' death, burial, and resurrection was God's way of throwing a "monkey wrench" into the plans of the devil for world-wide destruction.

The Cross was God's way of pushing the "reset button" on the lives of those who have decided to place their trust in Jesus. Satan is referred to as the accuser of the brethren *(Revelation 12:10, Zephaniah 3:1)* because his job has been to accuse us before God and remind us of our sins. He knows that if he can influence us into living a lifestyle that is contrary to God, then we would disqualify ourselves from the blessings that are in Christ. The enemy is very cunning and deceptive. He is very subtle in his approach to blind the minds of people and to keep them from coming into the truth of Jesus.

This approach can best be seen in Hollywood and within the film industry. No longer are the scary movies about killer sharks, serial killers, and vampires. They are now all about the demons, witchcraft and the spiritual realm of darkness. Hollywood has taken today's horror movies to a whole other extreme.

The content of these movies is not what bothers me. It is the inaccurate portrayal of the spiritual battle between the realm of light and darkness. Believing what you may see in these movies, it is easy for people to walk away and think that the enemy has the power and authority to challenge the power of God.

It usually goes like this. Someone becomes haunted and tormented by the spells of witchcraft or a demonic presence. Then they intentionally go to a priest who has some form of knowledge concerning what's tormenting them. Then the priest goes into a battle with these demons. The demons almost overtake the priest and the person being tormented. Eventually, these characters barely prevail over these demonic powers only to return to their normal lives.

True spiritual warfare doesn't look anything like these movies. For there is no struggle for power and dominance between God and the enemy. Paul says in *Romans 16:20, NKJV, "And the God of peace will crush Satan under your feet shortly."* Where there is no light, darkness will always win. Where there is light, it's no contest and darkness has no chance. You are now seated in a place of victory.

"And He (God the Father) put all things under His (Jesus the Son of God) feet, and gave Him (Jesus) to be head over all things to the

> *church, which is His body (Us, believers in Christ), the fullness of Him who fills all in all" (Ephesians 1:22-23, NKJV).*

To live a distinguished life in the Lord is to live a life of victory over the darkness of the enemy. Now you are to fight from victory instead of fighting from defeat. Think about this. Jesus is the head of our lives, and we collectively are His body. God has placed "all things" under the "feet" of His body, that's us.

What are the "all things" is what you may be asking? All things are the works and strategies of the enemy. All spirits and demonic influences are included in the "all things." All known and unknown sicknesses, and diseases would be included in the "all things." Every state of poverty, failure, and tragedy would be included in the "all things." The good news for God's people is that all of these things are now under our feet.

Often, we measure our stances in life by our circumstances instead of by His finished works. You may have felt like you have been beaten up, broken or barely surviving in life. Be mindful that His victory is your victory and your victory is in the Lord. You are more than just a survivor. God's will for you is that you do more than just endure in life.

In Jesus, we are "more than conquerors." To be "more than a conqueror" does not mean that you barely won, but that your victory was a landslide victory (using sports terminology). Jesus didn't barely win on the Cross and neither are we to barely win in life. Our lives are to reflect the conquest, triumph, and victory that was established for us through Jesus.

The Exchanged Life

If you have stayed with me up to this point, I know that you must be thinking, "This Gospel is too good to be true." This good news is true. So then you would say, "Surely there is a catch to this. Perhaps I must do something?" "Maybe I have to give God all of my money?" "Maybe I have to give up all of my time and visit the poor, the less fortunate and the sick?" "Or perhaps I have to give up all of my friendships, television shows, hobbies or dreams to have this good news." I preface my next statement by saying that I would never put it past the Lord for Him to ask you to do any of these things that were just mentioned. Especially when any of these things may threaten or challenge that place in your heart that God desires.

I will say that for us to truly experience the fullness of the Gospel, God is asking for us to give up our lives in exchange. For us to experience all that comes with the life of Jesus, we must first give up our lives unto Him. The beginning of His life and all of its blessings first begins with our willingness to see the end of our lives. It's when we are ready to fully relinquish all that we are unto God that we will begin to experience His life, benefits, and His finished works.

When the Gospel is preached, many people do not have a problem crying out to Jesus as their Savior. Many people do not have a problem acknowledging Him as the Son of God or the only way to Heaven. Where the rubber meets the road in our willingness to receive the Gospel, is in our willingness to acknowledge Him as Lord. Lord, being the one who is over all and runs all. Being Lord of our lives means that it is Jesus who is to have control over our lives.

Often, we still have difficulties surrendering to God. For many people, the most offensive part of the Gospel is that God requires us to give up our lives. It isn't always about whether we have said "yes" to Jesus, but rather have we been continuing to say "yes" unto the Lord? How many days has it been that we have continued to say "yes" to Him as Lord over our lives? Living distinguished is grounded in the fact that we have continued to say "yes" each day of our lives.

A few years ago when the automotive industry was looking to make a comeback, there were various car dealerships that were eager to sell you a new car in exchange for your current car. These dealerships did not care how old your car was or the mileage, damage or negative equity that was still owed on the car. They had a slogan that was simply, *"We accept all trade-ins."* The same is true with our Lord and Savior. No matter how old you are. No matter the mileage that you have accumulated. No matter your damage or the balance that you have run up in your life, Jesus is also willing to accept all trade-ins.

Imagine this with me. Let's say that you have decided to accept the offer that was made from these dealerships. You agreed to trade in your car for a brand new one. Instead of trading in your whole car, you decided to trade it in piece by piece to the dealership. This week you will give them the bumpers. Next week you would give them the tires. Perhaps the week after, you would decide to give them the steering wheel. Still expecting them to give you their new vehicle in its entirety.

How far would you get along with this type of negotiations? Not too far, right? So that you can drive off the lot with the new car, you must first be willing to give up the entirety of the old one. This is the type of negotiation that many believers have tried to run past God. Only to find out that with Him it is all or nothing. Let's not trade in our lives in increments, but let's wholly surrender our lives to Him in exchange for all that He has.

> *"To give them beauty for ashes, The oil of joy for mourning, The garment of praise for the spirit of heaviness" (Isaiah 61:3, NKJV). "Now all things are of God, who has reconciled us to Himself through Jesus Christ" (2 Corinthians 5:18, NKJV).*

Jesus took our mess, failures and sins to the Cross and made an exchange so that we may have His life and His goodness. This form of an exchange is a common theme throughout all of the scriptures. One of the meanings of the word "reconcile" in this passage is to "exchange." Through Jesus, God made provisions for the world and its sins to be exchanged for His grace. How was this provision and exchange made possible? Paul answers this question in verse 21. *"For He made Him who knew no sin to be sin for us, that we might become the righteousness of God in Him" (2 Corinthians 5:21, NKJV).*

For our shame, Jesus died so that we may have His honor. For our sadness and mourning, we now have His joy. For our rejection and confusion, we now have God's peace, and love. God knew that we could not save ourselves. So out of His unfailing love for us; He made provisions for our salvation. God has always been about making an exchange with His people. The question becomes, are we willing to make the exchange as well? Let's talk about how to make this exchange.

The Strategy for the Exchanged Life

> *"I have been crucified with Christ; it is no longer I who live, but Christ lives in me; and the life which I now live in the flesh I live by faith in the Son of God, who loved me and gave Himself for me. I do not set aside the grace of God; for if righteousness comes through the law, then Christ died in vain" (Galatians 2:20-21, NKJV).*

In this passage is the strategy for living the exchanged life. Verse 20 starts off with "I have been crucified with Christ." It is easy to acknowledge Jesus' death on the Cross. It is a whole other thing to acknowledge that we died with Him on that same Cross. His death was our death!

What this means is that to recognize His death, we must also recognize that He died in our place, and now our lives belong to him. "We have now been bought with a price" and all that we are belongs to the one who purchased our freedom. Many of us have not been able to accept His life and all that comes with it because we fail to accept our deaths.

Paul goes on to say that "it is no longer I who live, but Christ lives in me." To live a distinguished life is to embrace the fact that life is no longer about you being at the center. It is now Jesus who is at the center of everything. A distinguished life is to live an exchanged life. It is about knowing that your life is now hidden with Christ and that Jesus now desires to live His life within you.

Many of us are not experiencing God's quality of life because we aren't willing to give up our lives first. If our lives were like driving a car, too many times we refuse to relinquish the wheel over to Jesus. We continue to remain in the driver's seat of our lives, while we only allow Jesus to remain in the passenger's seat. One day we will have to switch seats and allow Jesus to take over the wheel. One day it will be Jesus who drive, direct and navigate our lives in the directions that we are to go. It's in *"Him that we are to live, move and have our beings" (Acts 17:28, NKJV).*

The Resurrected Life

Throughout the majority of this chapter, I have referenced the Gospel with the fact that Jesus went to the Cross. It would only be right that as I bring this chapter to a close that I end it with His resurrection. The Gospel may have started with the Cross, but the good news of Jesus is that He is no longer on the Cross. He has risen from the grave and is now seated at the right hand of God. We call this the resurrection of Jesus. This good news is relevant to us today because now His resurrection has also become our resurrection. As He was raised from the grave and the grips of death, so were we.

Essentially, a distinguished life is to live a resurrected life. It is to live a life where Jesus is living His life within us, and we are living out His resurrection. A distinguished life is one that has become signified and marked by the resurrection power of God. We have been raised up and resurrected from every dead situation. The thought of a resurrection is to acknowledge something or someone who was once dead but was raised up and restored to a new life. This resurrected life is now your testimony!

Living Out His Resurrection

The goal of the Gospel is not that we would learn to live a better, humbled, meek life and just survive until Jesus returns again. God's desire is not for His people to display His power by showing the world how to endure and barely make it through life. In fact, you can do this without Jesus. God's heart and desires are for us to become love to a hurting world. We are to become a light to those who are in darkness. We are to show mercy to a world that is full of condemnation.

Jesus has saved us and is alive within us to show the world an abundant life. The world should not just want what you have, but they should begin to desire the One that you have and the good news that comes with Him. When we begin to exchange our lives for His and walk into His resurrection power, learning to live distinguished will become easy. We will all see that living a distinguished life is the byproduct of the Gospel and Jesus' resurrected life. Life will become more than just trying to live for Jesus and more about allowing Him to live His life through you.

The Return of the King

In the summer of 2014 LeBron James, who at this time was the best basketball player in the NBA and arguably in the world, had decided to return home and to continue his basketball career in Cleveland. Being recognized in today's time as the King of Basketball, many people have called and crowned him as "King James." The headlines of various newspapers across this nation and throughout Cleveland read, "The Return of the King." The fans of Cleveland were elated with the good news of King James' return to the city. The entire city celebrated as he fulfilled his promise to bring them an NBA championship in the summer of 2016.

God's people should be even more excited at the thought of our King, the undisputed Champion, Jesus, and His second return to bring us to glory. The good news of Jesus doesn't just end at the Cross or even with His resurrection. This good news is that one day He will return for those who have entrusted their lives unto the Lord. The return of our King will be more than just the saving of a city, but it will be to establish His rule and reign on the earth. Until that day, let's be people who have received His good news, and lived out the Gospel before others as we prepare the way for the return of our King.

There is no way that someone could have read about all of God's goodness in Jesus without desiring to have a relationship with this amazing God. This first begins with believing that Jesus is the Son of God and that in Him we shall be accepted before God. It is not the repeating of a prayer that causes one to become "saved," but it is the fact that one has believed in his/her heart that Jesus is the Savior of the world. If you feel that your heart is at this place to relinquish your life over to Jesus, or you are not certain that you have ever fully given your life to the Lord, I would like to encourage you to make this prayer personal for yourself.

God, this day I choose to believe that Jesus is the Messiah and Savior of the world. No one comes to you but through Jesus. I believe that you love me and sent Jesus to die for my sins. I confess that I have lived a life apart from you and your ways, and I repent of all of my sins. This day, I choose to give my life to you and surrender all that I am to you. I thank you for saving me, and for forgiving me. I ask that you will fill me with your Spirit, and teach me how to follow you. Help me to realize who I am in you and all that Jesus finished for me on the Cross. This I pray in Jesus name, Amen!

3
Distinguished By Discipleship

Before the disciples decided to follow Jesus, they were known as untrained, uneducated, ordinary fisherman. After being with Jesus, they were extraordinary men who were used to change the world. What made the difference? In between the time, they had decided to follow Jesus. They had decided to become disciples of Jesus. Before Jesus, they were fishermen, but after Jesus, they became fishers of men, whose nets are still catching people today.

These men were called to fulfill a life of purpose and destiny. They were called to live a distinguished life, a life that would demonstrate the power and glory of God. They were called to introduce to the world a new way of living and the Kingdom of God. They were called to build, create and present to the world what would be known as the church. In essence, these ordinary men were called to change the course of history and bring people into the knowledge of Jesus as the Son of God.

Before they were called to live a life of greatness for Jesus, their first call was to come and to follow Jesus. Before they were leaders, they were followers. Jesus used these ordinary men to present to the world an extraordinary God. As we pursue our dreams to become preachers, athletes, entrepreneurs and entertainers, we must first answer the call to become followers of Jesus. Our call to significance for the Lord begins with our call to learn of Him and follow His teachings. As we aspire to chase after greatness, it is essential that we first learn to sit at the feet of the one who defines greatness, Jesus. If there is one person that Jesus is going to use to change the world, this person must first be a disciple.

> *"The next day Jesus decided to leave for Galilee. Finding Philip, he said to him, "Follow me" (John 1:43, NIV). "As Jesus was walking beside the Sea of Galilee, he saw two brothers; Simon called Peter and his brother Andrew. They were casting a net into the lake, for they were fishermen. "Come, follow me," Jesus said, "and I will send you out to fish for people." "At once they left their nets and followed him" (Matt 4:18-19, NIV). "Then Jesus said to Simon, "Don't be afraid; from now on you will fish for people." So they pulled their boats up on shore, left everything and followed him" (Luke 5:10-11, NIV).*

What's the recurring theme found in these passages? It wasn't the fact that Jesus first called these men to become pastors. It wasn't a call to a seminary school or to become a church member. Jesus' first call was for them to "follow him" and to be His disciples. Jesus was inviting them to observe Him and His works. They were to learn about Him and His teachings. Jesus was inviting these men into a relationship with Him that would transform them and fulfill their destinies. This call did not end with them, but instead, it still continues with us. There is still a call for a group of people that would be willing to leave everything behind and follow Him. There is a call for someone to join God in His work of spreading His Gospel and building His Kingdom.

To follow means to pay close attention to and to put into practice the teachings, instructions and ways of another person. To be a disciple means to be a learner of someone else's teachings and philosophies. A disciple is one who is willing to devote their lives to the teachings of another person with the hopes of spreading and demonstrating these teachings to others. Jesus was calling these men to learn, observe and put into practice His teachings of the Kingdom.

This call was with the expectation that He would one day use their lives to demonstrate the will and ways of God to everyone whose paths they would cross. Jesus still desires to use our lives today to demonstrate His principles and ways. God desires to use our lives to show the world a more superior way of living life. Our lives are what God wants to use to show the world the significance of His will and the power of His Word.

In this lifetime, we are all following something. It is safe to say that your life will always reflect what you believe in and what you are willing to follow. So if being a disciple means that we are to give our lives over to Jesus to learn, follow and exemplify His ways, then discipleship is the process in which God uses our lives to teach others how to follow Him. Discipleship is more than just a class and a course. It is when God's people are willing to live their lives with others with the intent of teaching them how to follow Jesus.

We have the greatest purpose and call in the world as God's people. We are called to prepare the way for Jesus' return. We are called to enforce His finished works, advance His Kingdom and spread His Gospel. We are called to change our neighborhoods and "turn the world upside down" for the Lord. We are to raise the standards of this world and to show the world true greatness. As people of God, we are to bring the impossibilities of life into this world. With all of these great calls that are from God, they all start first with the call to follow Jesus. When we are faithful to follow, He will be faithful to fulfill His plan for greatness within our lives.

No Fan Clubs

If the Gospel is the message of God that brings salvation, then discipleship is our response to that message. After hearing and learning of the goodness of God to send His Son Jesus to die on the Cross, who wouldn't want to forsake all to follow Him? The Gospel is our doctrine and being a disciple is our duty. To some people, the ways in which the disciples were called to follow Jesus seems outdated and old-fashioned. His call for followers is as true today as it was 2000 years ago.

In many of our communities, we are running the risk of making more fan clubs of Jesus instead of making disciples. Jesus is looking for disciples, not fans. A fan picks and chooses a sports team to root for, and when their team is striving to win these fans are there to cheer for them. This is great for those who are into sports or those who have a favorite entertainer. The problem with fans is that when their favorite teams begin to lose, they decide to no longer remain loyal to these teams.

Oftentimes, the loyalty of a team's fan base is contingent on the team's performances. This is the same with our commitment to Jesus. As long as He is holding up His end of the bargain, we will remain loyal fans of Jesus. With God, we have a "what have you done for me lately" mentality. The moment that He doesn't seem to do what we desire we consider jumping teams.

Many times our commitment is contingent on His performance in our lives. Almost like saving us isn't enough. I'd imagine that this is why it was said of Him that *"Jesus did not commit Himself to them because He knew all men" (John 2:24, NKJV)*. A disciple of Jesus is one who has made a sober decision to abandon all and to acknowledge Jesus as Lord and Savior. Their decision to follow Jesus isn't contingent on how they are feeling, whether they agree with God's will for their lives or how others may see them. They have come to realize that there is no other way to live apart from Jesus. In Him, there is life and in Him, that life is to be more abundantly.

In John chapter 6, there is a story of a multitude of people who decided to follow Jesus. Their decision to follow Him was because He had just performed a miracle of multiplying fish and bread. This miracle fed a multitude of people. When it came for them to learn about His ways and teachings, the people's response was, *"This is very hard to understand. How can anyone accept it?" (John 6:60, NLT)*. They followed Him for His miracles but rejected Him because of His message. They decided to no longer follow Jesus.

When asking the other disciples on whether they too were going to abandon Jesus and turn away from following Him, Peter's response was, *"Lord, to whom would we go? You have the words that give eternal life. We believe, and we know you are the Holy One of God" (John 6:68-69, NLT)*. The hearts of the people who turned away were not ready to receive the truths of Jesus' teachings. They were not able to discern who He was. It was Peter and the other disciples that realized that His words were "spirit and life" and that Jesus truly was the Son of God.

Fans may turn away after having to "count the cost" of being a disciple. Fans may reject Jesus after learning that they no longer are to dictate how they would like for their lives to turn out. It will be fans who will no longer decide to follow Jesus once they realize that His ways are not their ways. This degree of devotion is seen and played out throughout our communities each day as we often see people fall away from the faith. It is the followers who will continue to stick to the course and walk with Jesus on this journey called life.

In many instances, our decisions to accept Jesus as our Lord and Savior and to be His disciple is made out of emotions. It's usually after the climatic end of a sermon and once the band has played our favorite song that we will make this decision to come to Jesus. The only problem is that once our emotions wear off so does our commitment. We must be careful that we do not fall into this trap of making decisions and commitments to God out of our emotions. This decision to truly be a disciple of Jesus must be a conscious decision as we "count the cost" to follow Him. *"For which of you, intending to build a tower, does not sit down first and count the cost, whether he has enough to finish it"* (Luke 14:28, NKJV). The ultimate difference between being a fan and being a follower is having to "count the cost" when it comes to giving our lives over to God.

Carrying Our Cross

Our first call to God is to come and to follow Him. A major aspect of this call is the demand to "deny ourselves." This demand requires us to "carry our cross" and separates fans of Jesus from followers of Jesus. A fan celebrates that Jesus went to the Cross and died on that Cross for them. A follower recognizes that He didn't die by Himself on that Cross. Instead, they recognize that they died on that Cross with Him. Each day, the Cross serves as a reminder of what Jesus did, our death in Him and that to truly follow Him we must first deny ourselves.

It is a necessity that we "deny ourselves" daily because the only thing that can hinder God's move and promises within our lives is ourselves. To "deny ourselves" is to totally yield all that we are to God and to acknowledge that we are no longer in control of our lives. It is "no longer us who lives, but now it is Christ who lives in us." The significance of a disciple's life is that Jesus is now living His life through us. God knows that we cannot do this each day in our strength for flesh will never deny flesh. To help us each day He has given us a Cross to carry.

> *"Those who belong to Christ Jesus have nailed the passions and desires of their sinful nature to his cross and crucified them there"* (Galatians 5:24, NLT). In the next chapter Paul pens, *"As for me, may I never boast about anything except the cross of our Lord Jesus Christ. Because of that cross, my interest in this world has been crucified, and the world's interest in me has also died"* (Galatians 6:14-15, NLT).

Paul here declares that the only thing that he has worth bragging about was the very Cross of Christ. At the Cross, his desires and interest for the world were destroyed, and the world's interest in him was also destroyed.

In our attempts to achieve greatness and live a distinguished life in the Lord, we must come to the realization that our call isn't to be impressed with the world, but to be used by God to save the world. If we chose not to surrender ourselves to God, we would begin to follow the ways of the world. We will eventually strive to become more like our favorite athletes, entertainers, and celebrities. We will strive to become more like them and less like Jesus. But the Cross crucifies our desires of the world and the world's desires for us. Whenever we become impressed with the entertainment, fame and fortune, we will run the risk of compromising God's call to being disciples and His message of redemption.

Nowadays, it has become easy to carry a convenient Cross that requires no commitment. The association with a cross seem to be accepted and more popular than with Christ Himself. In fact, you can find Crosses everywhere: displayed on t-shirts, bumper stickers, jewelry selections, billboards and even tattooed on body parts. The Cross that Jesus told us to carry to truly follow Him was never intended to be on our shirts, but rather to be carried on our backs.

To carry our Cross is to be more than just having a t-shirt or a bumper sticker that affiliates ourselves with Jesus. It is a mindset in which Jesus is a reality, and our commitment and decision to follow Him is a lifestyle. To carry our Crosses is to have a mindset that true victory is only experienced when I have decided to no longer be the center of my universe. It is when I have given up my life to Jesus that He may be my Lord, the center of all that I am. It is when we continue to hold onto our lives that we actually lose it (Luke 17:33). When we finally decide to trust God with our lives more than we trust ourselves, we will truly begin to experience His life.

"And they overcame him because of the blood of the Lamb and because of the word of their testimony" (Revelation 12:11, NASB).

This is one passage that I have always heard quoted and celebrated amongst many believers which by all means should be celebrated. I never really heard the rest of this particular passage recited. The rest of the passage would go on to read like this, *"and they did not love their lives to the death."* Specifically, who was this that had *"overcome by the blood of the Lamb?"* It was those who did not *"love their own lives unto death."* It was people who found more satisfaction and reward in being willing to give up their lives and in exchange they were the ones who would experience the victory of Jesus.

The Cross of Jesus is the only place where you can experience the essence of His life by first experiencing your death. It is as we carry our Cross as disciples that the works of Jesus will begin to distinguish us, set us apart and define our significance in life. No longer will we stand in the way of our progress or be the reason why we were never able to maximize our fullest potential in life. The Cross is God's way of moving us out of the way so that He may show Himself and His ways within us.

The irony of the Cross is that the very thing that is designed to humble us and cause us to deny ourselves is the very thing that also qualifies us for God's promises. The entryway to God's Kingdom and purposes is by way of the Cross. There is no other way to enter into God's world. It is what Jesus accomplished at the Cross that qualified us for the blessings of God. God's acceptance of us was predicated on Jesus dying on our behalf. The countless tangible promises that God has for us in this lifetime was solely established because of the shed blood of Jesus.

Giving, sowing and reaping are all great Biblical principles that work, but they are not a substitute for the Cross. Making Biblical and prophetic declarations are great disciplines to develop, but they are not substitutes for the works of the Cross. Attending church services and fellowshipping with other believers are great aspects of our faith. They in themselves are no substitutes for the works of the Cross. In fact, these are principles that work only because of the finished works of Jesus. They are principles that are set into motion and have been activated to work from the Cross. These principles will only go as far as your revelation of the Cross. They are not to serve as a substitute for the Cross and the means to earn God's blessings.

We must come to the revelation that the only reason God has considered to bless us is that His Son took our sins to the Cross. It is the Cross of Jesus and having been raised up to a "new life" in the Lord. In James B. Richard's book, *"How to Stop the Pain"*, he says, *"In order for God to even consider blessing us as a result of our efforts, He would have to completely deny the finished work of His Son. Looking for ways to earn or obtain blessings always causes us to look someplace other than the Lord Jesus and His finished works."* The Cross is to remind us of the blessings that we are to obtain now because of the Lord. A life of greatness and significance starts with a call to become disciples of Jesus. A disciple's life means nothing without his Cross. A distinguished life is a life that is marked by the Cross.

A Cross with No Power

Knowing Jesus and what He accomplished on the Cross is more than enough to distinguish you in life. When we use our education, social status, and wealth to distinguish us, we then run the risk of being disciples who are now proclaiming a powerless Cross. *"For Christ did not send me to baptize, but to preach the gospel— not with wisdom and eloquence, lest the cross of Christ be emptied of its power" (1 Corinthians 1:17, NIV).*

Here in this passage is a principle and a warning to all who aspire to be used by God for greatness. We should never allow our natural wisdom, skills, ability, eloquence or philosophies to be what we use for effectiveness in the Lord. The warning is that when we do we end up emptying the Cross of its power. Instead of ministering a Cross that brings transformation to those that are around us, we end up ministering a Cross that is powerless. This powerless Cross is because we have come to trust in our abilities over His works. A powerless Cross is one that can shout the people in our Sunday services, but it lacks the power to save them.

When we are truly carrying our Crosses and allowing the Cross to have its way, we will see God's power at work in our lives. When we no longer decide to compromise the true message of God and His Gospel, our lives will become the example of the power of the Cross and the message that has transcended time. Instead of denying God's power, we should become a people who have denied ourselves and then we will show the world the power of the Cross. A life of being set apart for significance must first be established in our willingness to carry our Crosses and remain true followers of Jesus.

Devoted Only To Him

Throughout the four Gospels, Jesus demanded the disciple's commitment. This degree of devotion was evident. He left no room for us today to ever guess how serious and important it was to Jesus for His people to relentlessly follow Him. No other passages bring this to light than that of Luke 9:58-62 and Matthew 10:37-39. Let's take a look.

"And Jesus said to him, "Foxes have holes and birds of the air have nests, but the Son of Man has nowhere to lay His head." Then He said to another, "Follow Me." But he said, "Lord, let me first go and bury my father." Jesus said to him, "Let the dead bury their own dead, but you go and preach the kingdom of God." And another also said, "Lord, I will follow You, but let me first go and bid them farewell who are at my house." But Jesus said to him, "No one, having put his hand to the plow, and looking back, is fit for the kingdom of God" (Luke 9:58-62, NKJV).

At first, it appears as if Jesus is making it difficult to follow Him. Instead, Jesus is painting a clear picture of what is expected to follow Him.

"He who loves father or mother more than Me is not worthy of Me. And he who loves son or daughter more than Me is not worthy of Me. And he who does not take his cross and follow after Me is not worthy of Me. He who finds his life will lose it, and he who loses his life for My sake will find it" (Matthew 10:37-39, NKJV).

Once again, it appears as if Jesus is attempting to make it difficult to be His disciple, but this is not the case. He is explaining the expectations of what it means to follow Him. In no means would God ever expect you to dishonor your family and parents. In comparison to your devotion to your family, parents, friends and loved ones, our devotion to Him should be unparalleled. We should be mindful that God desires not to take a back seat to anyone.

"Being devoted to something means being focused on that particular thing almost exclusively. When you are devoted to a cause, you work to achieve its goals. When you are devoted to a person, you place their needs above your own" (Vocabulary.com). With this being so apparent throughout the Gospels, it should begin to make us all wonder why this level of commitment is no longer expected from us today. I'd imagine that as intense as Jesus was 2000 years ago, He would have the same intensity in what our commitment should be to Him. His requirements haven't changed. In a time where it has become so normal to have more fans than followers, it shouldn't come to us as a surprise that the standards of following Him have been lowered.

We as believers of Jesus will often express more of an allegiance to our careers than we would our relationships with Him. People have shown more allegiance to their sororities, fraternities, social clubs and lodges than they have being followers of Jesus. Anything that causes you to pledge an allegiance to something other than God is not of God. Anything that requires an absolute commitment to its rules or secretive commitments is likely not to be God's will for your life.

Now, I am not saying that being a disciple means that you are to disassociate yourself from the rest of the world. What I am saying is that anything that requires your undivided commitment will ultimately deter you away from being a follower of Jesus. Too many times people have publically display their allegiance to a social club or lodge yet still struggle with their devotion and walk with Jesus. If you are struggling in a consistent walk with the Lord, then everything else should take the backseat until your walk has been strengthened, including every other commitment and relationship.

If Jesus had a fraternity, perhaps it would be called "Discipleship." Instead of pledging to get in, one would need to give their lives to Him in order to be a part of His fraternity. This is the fraternity that we should desire to belong to with others. Not one that would cause us to vacillate in our commitment to it and our commitment to Him. Anything that requires your allegiance will serve as an influence in how you live, what you think and what you do for the Lord. Jesus said *"No one can serve two masters; for either he will hate the one and love the other, or he will be devoted to one and despise the other" (Matthew 6:24, NASB).*

There are so many things that are subtly fighting for your devotion. Jesus is letting us know that it is impossible to be devoted to Him and something else, whether it be our jobs, careers, businesses, friendships, churches, or relationships. When trying to be devoted to these things and Jesus, we will be committed to one and "despise" the other one. We will either be devoted to Jesus, making our other relationships and commitments take the back seat to Him, or we will place these other things before the Lord.

In other countries, when someone decides to follow Jesus, it becomes a true reality for them to count the cost. In Indonesia, Iraq and Iran as people are coming to Jesus daily by the hundreds, they are mindful that giving their lives to Jesus will cause them to be rejected by family. In China, as they huddle together in their secret churches, it is a reality to them that every day could be their last day. Their government has become relentless in putting a stop to the spread of the Gospel in their country. What's amazing is that despite the measure of persecution, to many of them these threats, dangers and persecutions have not caused them to waiver in their devotion to God.

To them, making an allegiance to anything other than Jesus would defeat the purpose of why they are risking their lives to be His followers. It's only here in America where it has become the norm to simultaneously call ourselves Christians and pledge ourselves with other things. In fact, God is not looking for Baptist Christians, COGIC Christians, Presbyterian or Lutheran Christians. Instead, He is looking for true followers. He desires followers whose devotion isn't to a certain denomination or fellowship, but to Jesus alone. A disciple's devotion is one of no question, and their devotion to the Lord is one that should set the standard for others that are around them.

Following His Teachings

God desires to use your life to show the world His glory. This display of glory is done and established through us His people in a variety of ways. One of the primary ways is through His word. It was the Apostle John who said that Jesus was the word, and the *"Word became flesh and dwelt among us" (John 1:14, NKJV)*. Essentially, these disciples walk with the Word. They saw the Word of God (Jesus) perform miracles, heal the sick, raise the dead and even be proclaimed with authority. I would say that what they learned the most by walking with the "Word" day in and day out was the very nature, character, plans, and will of God.

If there was any one group that was prepared to know who God was and to carry out His will, it was the disciples. We shouldn't envy them now just because they were able to walk physically with Jesus. Today we have that same privilege and opportunity to walk with Jesus, learn of God, and follow His teachings. He left us His Spirit to be with us and His Word that is still among us. Jesus was the "Word that became flesh" while today we are to be flesh that is designed to become the Word.

A distinguished life lived before others is one that has become the example of God's truths and ways. When I say the "Word," I'm not referring to a leather bound book that is filled with historical figures and stories. I am referring to God's living word that was inspired by His Spirit. This "Word" is still alive today to bring life and transformation to us all.

Today, we can walk with Jesus and follow Him by allowing His word to be the authoritative figure in our lives. We should not attempt to conform His word to fit and apply to our lives. Instead, we should allow His word to conform our lives to His ways. There is no way that one could ever say that they truly know who Jesus is without discovering His nature, existence, and ways through His word.

This was the case for the disciples as they walked with the "Word" on a daily basis, and if it worked for them, then it should still work for us now. *"And you shall know the truth, and the truth shall make you free" (John 8:32, NKJV).* Many times we have quoted this passage without actually seeing it come to fruition in our lives. I would like to suggest that the secret to this passage becoming a reality in our lives is in the passage right before it, verse 31. *"Then Jesus said to those Jews who believed Him, "If you abide in My word, you are My disciples indeed."*

Jesus tells His disciples that if they would remain faithful to His word and all that He had taught them, then they would "know the truth, and the truth shall make them free." A society that has become alienated from God's word and teachings will become a society that will not experience the true freedom of God. Living a life of significance is learning to live a life of freedom. True freedom comes by way of being Jesus' disciples and "abiding in His word."

Just as Jesus was the face of the Father, we are now to be the face of Jesus on earth. People will come to know the true nature of Jesus as they examine our lives. As we learn to follow God's teachings through His word, we will begin to be the very image of God on earth. The call of a disciple is to make visible the invisible God in our communities, families, jobs and careers. The old cliché has been that people would rather "see a sermon any day than hear one." God's desire has always been to prove Himself and to use our lives as an example of His word and His ways.

"Clearly, you are an epistle of Christ, ministered by us, written not with ink but by the Spirit of the living God, not on tablets of stone but on tablets of flesh, that is, of the heart" (2 Corinthians 3:3, NKJV). The call of a disciple and a distinguished life is to be what Paul calls an "epistle of Christ." A very letter written by God to be read by the lives that are around us. Our lives will always bear witness and testify to something whether we know it or not. It's better to be a witness to the truth and the ways of God than to be a witness to the ways of the world.

This letter from God is no longer just to be by ink and printed on paper or tablets of stone, but now it is to be written on our hearts by God's Spirit. God is within you to write His word onto your hearts. When people come to know more of who you are, they should also begin to learn more of who God is and His goodness within your life. When people are around you, what is it about God that they learn? What truths has your life been the example of that would make people want to learn more about Jesus? As we come to follow Jesus and His teachings, it will become inevitable that people will begin to see His very life and nature within us.

His Teachings Alone

To follow His teachings means that God's word has to be the most influential aspects of our lives. We cannot have a mixture in our understandings of God. God's living word holds practical principles to our everyday lives. There will never be a circumstance that His word hasn't already addressed and provided practical strategies for our situations. When we fail to learn from His word and follow His teachings, we will become influenced to go outside of Jesus to get answers to life.

> *"In him (Jesus) lie hidden all the treasures of wisdom and knowledge. I am telling you this so no one will deceive you with well-crafted arguments." "Don't let anyone capture you with empty philosophies and high-sounding nonsense that come from human thinking and from the spiritual powers of this world, rather than from Christ"* (Colossians 3:3-4, 8, NLT).

In Jesus lies all of the truths and principles that we will ever need in life. In Him lies all of the wisdom and strategies that we will ever need to be set apart for greatness. In His living word lies all of the principles that are necessary for you to live a victorious life in Christ. When we fail to realize what we have "in Him," we will likely go outside of Him for "wisdom and knowledge." God's Gospel and His teachings do not need any additional assistance from today's top authors, scholars, and philosophers. His word is more than enough for us all.

Jesus was the most successful person who has ever walked the face of the earth. Learning to live like Him will always exceed the success and motivation that the world can ever provide. I am persuaded that the Bible is more than enough to experience the quality of life that God has destined for us. God's quality of life is to be best experienced as we learn to live life together with others.

Fellowship and Family

At the heart of discipleship is the call to fellowship. In fact, discipleship isn't just a call to walk with Jesus, but it is also a call to walk with others. God placed a natural desire in people to share their lives with others. I'd like to believe that the intention of this engrained desire to connect to others and belong was so that God would have a family amongst Himself. This family would help others to feel accepted in the Lord as well. Also, that there would be a community of people who would collectively work together to fulfill God's will. It was always designed that as disciples we would form a family that would serve as a model for true fellowship here on earth.

The Greek word for this form of fellowship is "Koinonia," meaning the greatest form of fellowship that a group of people may have with each other. We must not confuse this form of fellowship with our usual Sunday service gatherings. As great and necessary as these gatherings are, this form of fellowship is best seen after the services, and outside of the four walls of our churches. This degree of fellowship and existence is only accomplished with Jesus being at the center of this community. Imagine a place where people can come together to share their lives and encourage others. A place where people can come as they are, be accepted as they are, and not masquerade themselves to be someone that they are not. Instead, they can feel free to be open about their mistakes, failures, and insecurities. Everyone wants a place like this, and this place was always supposed to be amongst God and His people.

A disciple of Jesus understands the significance of fellowship and community. If you are someone who wants to live a distinguished life, you must come to understand that there are no "Lone Rangers" in the Kingdom of God. The Kingdom of God is a family business and in all that God does in the earth, He does it through His children. We should never desire to win in life by ourselves, but we must come to realize that life is a team sport that we are to win together.

Being One

> *"I do not pray for these alone, but also for those who will believe in Me through their word; that they all may be one, as You, Father, are in Me, and I in You; that they also may be one in Us, that the world may believe that You sent Me. And the glory which You gave*

> *Me I have given them, that they may be one just as We are one: I in*
> *them, and You in Me; that they may be made perfect in one, and*
> *that the world may know that You have sent Me, and have loved*
> *them as You have loved Me" (John 17:20-23, NKJV).*

Here is Jesus praying a prayer to His Father for us. Jesus acknowledges the fact that He and the Father were "One" and then He begins to pray that we, His followers today would be "one" as well. In the eyes of God, true fellowship is seen as being one with each other. True fellowship is being on one accord, one minded, and united in our hearts for the things of God. Jesus' intentions for His people to be "one" with each other was for a specific and important purpose.

"That they may be made perfect in one, and that the world may know that You have sent Me, and have loved them as You have loved Me" (John 17:23, NKJV). The first reason was so that the world may know that Jesus is the Son of God, who was sent to redeem the world. In this prayer is a significant truth in which we should remain mindful. He prayed that we would be "one" with each other. It would be this form of fellowship that God would use to validate the fact that Jesus was and is the Son of God. The fact that so many different cultures, backgrounds, and communities can come together as "one" will show the world that Jesus is our only hope for true redemption.

Secondly, His disciples being "one" with each other would best display God's love for the world. How amazing is that? Who would know that God would place so much weight on our willingness to put aside our differences and come together in Jesus? As a disciple of the Lord, we must realize that it is not enough to walk with Jesus only. It is our walk with Jesus that determines our walk with others. In fact, how we fellowship with others will always be a reflection of our relationship with the Lord. In living a distinguished life, you will never treat the Lord any better than how you treat the people who are around you.

One By His Spirit

As we just discovered the significance of being "one" with others. We should never make the mistake of believing that we can achieve this kind of fellowship in our own strength. In history, whenever we have attempted to unite to this degree, in our best efforts we have only divided. We have divided families. We have turned communities into cliques and churches into segregated circles. Whenever man tries to unite with others on his own, he will always run the risk of compromising God's purposes for unity. It is by the leading of God's Spirit that we can put aside our differences and come together as "one."

> *"Make every effort to keep yourselves united in the Spirit, binding*
> *yourselves together with peace. For there is one body and one Spirit,*
> *just as you have been called to one glorious hope for the future"*
> *(Ephesians 4:3-4, NLT).*

This one "glorious hope" that we are to have together in the Lord, and this peace that we are to be bound together in, is accomplished as we are "united in the Spirit." It is God's Spirit that unites us, keeps us united and causes us to fulfill God's purposes in this world.

Remember that it was in Acts chapter 2 that the disciples were being filled in an upper room at Pentecost. The chapter begins with the outpouring of God's Spirit and it ends with a community of people coming together as one in the Lord. *"Now all the believers were together and held all things in common" (Acts 2:44, NLT).* This is the order for true unity. First, we must be yielded to God and His Spirit personally; then it is Him who will unite us as one corporately.

As a disciple, in order for us to live a distinguished life, we must be mindful that our pursuit to follow Jesus begins with our willingness to be led by His Spirit. It is His Spirit that shall guide us into divine fellowship and lead us to remain united in the Lord. Jesus is the head and the center of this body. His Spirit is the nucleus of this body, and He is also the glue that keeps and holds us together as a people.

Filling the Void

God has placed within every human being a desire and longing to be accepted. The unity of the church as a family was to be the ultimate form of fellowship expressed on earth. This sense of belonging and acceptance would be fulfilled as people would come to live life with God and others. When we fail to be this unified collective unit, then there lies a void within the hearts of so many people for acceptance and true fellowship. When we fail to be "One" together in the Lord, the longing for a true sense of community continues to go unfulfilled.

Today we live in a world where being connected has become one of our top priorities in life. Social media and social networking have also become a billion-dollar industry. It has found a way for people to connect with and live their lives with others. Within every city and community, there are street gangs that are recruiting young people simply because the young people have a need to identify themselves through their affiliations. Fraternities, sororities, lodges, and clubs have all benefited from the fact that everyone is in need of a place where they can be identified with and acknowledged. Dating sites are flourishing because the establishing and maintaining of healthy relationships are at an all-time low. I believe that the church is God's design to model successful relationships and the foundations for healthy families.

We should never use our friendships and associations to define us or take the place in knowing that God defines our identities. Ultimately, every search for meaning and purpose ends with God. God fills the empty voids in our lives for fellowship and belonging. As we see God bring His people together to be "one" with each other, we will also begin to see homes restored. We will begin to experience peace within our streets. We will see families be made whole, differences in cultures reconciled and so many others come to know the love of God that is found through Jesus.

The Commission

> *"And Jesus came and spoke to them, saying, "All authority has been given to Me in heaven and on earth. Go therefore and make disciples of all the nations, baptizing them in the name of the Father and of the Son and of the Holy Spirit, teaching them to observe all things that I have commanded you; and lo, I am with you always, even to the end of the age" (Matthew 28:18-20, NKJV).*

He commissions them and tells them to "Go" and to "make disciples." Notice that He didn't say, "stand still" or just "live your life until you make it to Heaven." Instead, He charges these disciples to go make disciples. It is not enough to just be a disciple of Jesus, but the whole goal of a follower of Jesus is to make disciples as well.

At the heart of discipleship is the call to multiply. In fact, the very first blessing pronounced upon humanity was to *"Be fruitful and multiply" (Genesis 1:22, NKJV).*

When I say multiply, I mean that we are to teach others how to follow Jesus as we have been taught how to follow Him. *"Imitate me, just as I also imitate Christ" (1 Corinthians 11:1, NKJV)*. It is God's will to use your life as the means by which He teaches others how to be His disciples.

As we develop a heart to make disciples, we will begin to see people as God sees them. In every person is the ability to reach a greater number of people. We will have an effective influence for God within our neighborhoods and communities. Oftentimes, when we see someone, we see them as one person, and we may overlook the potential that God has deposited in their lives. We limit the influence that God has given them for His Kingdom. Inside every person is a community that they are assigned to with the potential to multiply and to make disciples for the Lord.

Avery T Willis, Jr. once said in his book called "*The Master's Life*" that, *"Many people count the number of apples on a tree, but few see the numbers of trees in an apple. The real fruit of an apple is the future trees that grow from its seeds."* Within every apple are multiple seeds that have the potential to become trees of its own. Inside of every disciple is the ability to effect the lives of so many others. No matter their credentials, education, accolades or the lack thereof, God will guide them to draw others to Himself and to make disciples. We must come to believe in the multiplying power that God has placed within us so that we may make disciples for God and change the world that is around us. This all begins with a call to follow Him and a commission to spread His Gospel.

By This, They Shall Know

A disciple is something that people shall come to recognize you to be. There should be something about your walk before others that lets them know that you are a follower of Jesus. There should be something about your character and demeanor that sets you apart. What is this "something" that should be noticeable to other people?

> *"A new commandment I give to you, that you love one another; as I have loved you, that you also love one another. By this all will know that you are My disciples, if you have love for one another" (John 13:34-35, NKJV)*.

73

What was it that Jesus says that others will know that you are one of His disciples? Love. That's right! By how we are able to demonstrate God's love unto others, is how others will come to know that we belong to God. This is important to know as we desire to grow in the Lord and learn to live a distinguished life. This is accomplished first by our receptivity to receive His love and then and only then will we be able to love others. If Jesus is the standard and epitome of greatness, then our lives should always reflect greatness. If Jesus is the mark of a distinguished life, then as we follow Him, so shall our lives be a reflection of living distinguished.

4

Distinguished By His Spirit

M ore often than not, when a woman experiences symptoms such as a change in her appetite, food cravings, fatigue, and early morning nausea, she then begins to question the possible conception of a child. These are common symptoms that many women experience in a potential pregnancy. In essence, whenever there is new life growing inside of you, there will always be evidence. This new life within you changes everything about the life you knew beforehand. For those who profess to be believers in Jesus, this truth should be all too real for them as well.

As life changing as this is, how much more should the Holy Spirit living within God's people also be? After Jesus' ascension, it was His Spirit that descended and was poured out onto the followers of Jesus. When there is the pregnancy of a child, there will eventually be signs and evidence that not only confirms to the mother that she is expecting, but also to others that she is carrying a new life within her.

This may not have been the experiences for all expecting women, but for my wife, one of the first signs of pregnancy was that her appetite changed drastically. What once fulfilled her appetite and cravings, she no longer desired. Many of her favorite foods would make her sick and nauseated. These old desires were then replaced with new desires, cravings, and appetites.

As God's Spirit begins to live within us, we too will no longer desire the cravings of old things. Old habits and old desires will no longer do. We have now begun to crave new desires, new habits, and dreams. We have been led by God to live a new lifestyle that only comes from Him.

It is normal and healthy throughout the pregnancy to experience the stretching. This stretching isn't always comfortable. The more that we connect to the life of the Holy Spirit within us, we too will find ourselves being spiritually stretched beyond our comfort zones. We will experience growth in ways that we could have never imagined.

When there is new life within you, there should always be some sense of evidence. When God has placed His Spirit within you, this new life of God will always place a demand for change. Transformation becomes evident in every area of our lives. No aspect of our lives and who we are should remain the same. Living a life of purpose is when we learn to embrace the Holy Spirit's presence and influence. A distinguished life is one where we have come to embrace this new life that God has placed within us by way of the Holy Spirit.

Who Is The Holy Spirit?

In both of the times when my wife was pregnant with our boys Landon and Langston, we would do all that we could to get acquainted with them and learn more about them. Even through the ultrasounds, we would try to gain as much insight as we could about what they would look like or what their personalities would be. Unless you intentionally wanted to be surprised, I'd imagine that you too would want to know who was living on the inside of you. I'd imagine that this must be the case with the Holy Spirit as well. As you are filled and led by the Holy Spirit, I would greatly suggest that you come to learn who this is that is living within you.

He is our source of life! It is sad to say that for many people we choose to never get acquainted with the source of this new life. We never come to experience the fullness of His presence. Many people would rather gather some brochures, books and teachings to understand who the Holy Spirit is. Instead of having a personal encounter with Him. So the question becomes, "Who is the Holy Spirit?" Who is this that is now living within you?" Let's start off with some basic but pertinent truths.

For starters, the Holy Spirit is not an "it," a "thing" or a "something." Rather, He is a person. As much of a person as we are. Some would reference Him as the "third person of the Trinity." Trinity being one God in the form of three persons. God as Father, God as Jesus the Son and God as the Holy Spirit.

He has many attributes and ways in which God's people have accurately described Him. He is known as our Comforter, (John 14:26) the One, who comforts us in the moments of turmoil and distress. He is our Spirit of liberty (2 Corinthians 3:17). In His presence there is freedom. He brings about the practical manifestation of God's grace in a believer's life (Hebrews 10:29).

He is known as our "seal" (2 Corinthians 1:22). The One, who has sealed and affirmed us in our salvation in the Lord. There are so many ways to experience Him and perceive Him in your life. Therefore, I would like to introduce who the Holy Spirit is in a disciple's life and not just give a theological discourse on His nature.

First off, He is simply the Spirit of God. I know that this may not be a mind-blowing revelation, but I do feel that we have often overcomplicated the person-hood and theology of the Holy Spirit. It was Jesus who revealed to us that *"God is Spirit" (John 4:24, NKJV)*. Not only must we come to *"worship Him in Spirit and in truth,"* but we must come to know God by His Spirit. You cannot have a relationship with God without experiencing and knowing His Spirit. There are many individuals who would claim to know God, but yet they would deny the practical existence of the Holy Spirit in their lives.

Certain theological teachings may actually teach against His current day existence. These teachings may lead someone to believe in the saving power of Jesus and the unconditional love of God the Father. Still, they may deny the true reality of the Holy Spirit here and now. This denial of God's Spirit is a true tragedy amongst us today. I have come with some good news—the Holy Spirit is alive and well! He is here on earth now.

He is God and as much of God as Jesus. He is not God junior or a third of God. The Holy Spirit is 100% God. In fact, Jesus said that it was good that He would go so that another would come (John 16:7). This "another" was and is the Holy Spirit.

When Jesus walked this earth in an earthly body that was God's strategy of connecting with men. It is His Spirit that is amongst us now. It is the Holy Spirit by which God now connects with, communicates with, draws into a relationship with and empowers people for His use. I'd like to believe that the Holy Spirit is the "how to" of God. If you would like to know how God moves, interacts and blesses His people, just know that He always does so by His Spirit. If you would like to know how you are to live a life of significance, purpose and destiny, we do so by God's Spirit.

His Job in Our Lives

The Holy Spirit is also the One in our lives who truly points us back to Jesus and transforms us day by day more into His image. When man leans to his own understanding, we end up with where we are now. That is, we end up with a thousand different doctrines, theologies, and denominations. Some believing that Jesus is the Son of God, while others believe that He was simply a prophet. Some believing that He was simply just a good man. How do we end up with so many different perspectives of one person? This is all a result of not yielding to the Holy Spirit, whose job is to point us back to Jesus.

He is also to guide us into all of the truths of Jesus. *"However, when He, the Spirit of truth, has come, He will guide you into all truth" (John 16:13, NKJV).* Apart from the revelation from God's Spirit, we have no clue who Jesus is. It will become inevitable that we will have a million different views of Jesus. It is God's Spirit that teaches us the true teachings of Jesus.

> *"But we all, with unveiled face, beholding as in a mirror the glory of the Lord, are being transformed into the same image from glory to glory, just as by the Spirit of the Lord" (2 Corinthians 3:18, NKJV).*

The Holy Spirit's job in our lives is to transform us into the image of Jesus. It is God's Spirit in our lives that reflects the true nature and Glory of God. Our lives are to reflect God's Glory. It is also His Spirit that points people back to God through our lives.

Ultimately, it is His job to live out and manifest the life of Jesus within us. It is not God's desire that you would just learn how to live like Jesus and cause your life to become a replica of His only. As the Holy Spirit now dwells within you, God will now begin to live out His life through you. Jesus' life didn't end at the Cross, nor is He up in Heaven idly waiting to return to earth. He is all too busy continuing to live His resurrected life through yours.

"I have been crucified with Christ; it is no longer I who live, but Christ lives in me" (Galatians 2:20, NKJV).

God desires for the world to see a new life manifested through you. You are now to become the walking billboard of Heaven on earth. Jesus finished His part on the Cross, and this was best illustrated when He said: "it is finished." God still has some business in the earth realm to carry out, and He wants to use your life to do so. As God's Spirit lives in you, you are now the epitome of what it looks like to be pregnant with purpose and potential. He is not in us for others to see what we can do in life; rather He is in us so that they may experience Him in all that we do.

"Because God from the beginning chose you for salvation through sanctification by the Spirit and belief in the truth" (2 Thessalonians 2:13, NKJV). "That I might be a minister of Jesus Christ to the Gentiles, ministering the gospel of God, that the offering of the Gentiles might be acceptable, sanctified by the Holy Spirit" (Romans 15:16, NKJV).

Both of these passages reveal to us that it is the Holy Spirit that "sanctifies" us. To sanctify means to cause something to be set apart, *"cleansed, consecrated and separated from profane things and dedicated to God."* It is God's Spirit at work within us who distinguishes us and sets us apart for God's will in our lives. Living a distinguished life is the result of remaining yielded to the work and leading of the Holy Spirit.

We must realize that we cannot set ourselves apart. No matter what your accomplishments in life may be, these things will never serve as a substitute for the Holy Spirit. Regardless of your education, it will have to be the leading of God's presence that makes the difference. *"For your presence among us sets your people and me apart from all other people on the earth" (Exodus 33:16, NLT).* The Holy Spirit is our sanctifier. It is His presence that sets us apart in this world. It was always God's intention to fill men with His distinguishing presence and make us His permanent dwelling place.

Today's Temple

In the Old Testament, God was seen as dwelling above man in Heaven and eventually in the tabernacles that were made by the hands of men. Throughout the Gospel, God was then seen walking amongst men through Jesus. We have now been ushered into a new dispensation where God is finally able to dwell in the lives and the hearts of men. God always desired a place where He could rest amongst His people.

> *"The Word became flesh and dwelt among us, and we beheld His glory" (John 1:14, NKJV).*

The word "dwell" means to be one's tabernacle. In other words, it is in the Gospels that we see Jesus being the tabernacle of God on wheels. Everywhere He went, God also went with Him. Jesus was the embodied presence of God moving throughout the earth. His life was an example of God's ultimate desire to make His people His permanent dwelling place.

> *"Do you not know that you are the temple of God and that the Spirit of God dwells in you?" (1 Corinthians 3:16, NKJV).*

Today, by way of God's Spirit, we are now God's tabernacles and temples. When others come into your presence they, in all actuality, should be experiencing the fullness of God's presence. You are now the embodiment of God's dwelling place. Those around you should not have to look far to get to God.

Due to a lack of understanding, we are still limiting God to a physical building when it is no longer the edifices of brick and mortar that God desires to dwell in. I have heard so many people say, "If I could just get my loved ones to a church, maybe they could get saved." If we only knew that we are the church and the saving power of God's presence was among us, then we would see our families come to experience God's grace for themselves when around us.

Even when we begin to pray for God to fill the temple in our church services, we look for a tangible manifestation of God's presence to fill the building. The whole time we miss the fact that this is the wrong temple that He is trying to fill. It is you that He wants to fill. God longs to use your life to display His Glory before others.

When we fail to know these truths, we will fall into the trap of esteeming the wrong tabernacles and committing our lives to building the wrong temples. The temples that we were designed to build were not buildings, but instead, we were to build up the lives of others. The more that we come to acknowledge the true blessing of being God's dwelling places, the more that we will come to appreciate our lives better as His temples. Just remember, you are the temple that God wants to fill!

> *"In the year that King Uzziah died, I saw the Lord sitting on a throne, high and lifted up, and the train of His robe filled the temple"* *(Isaiah 6:1, NKJV).*

What was God doing? He was sitting on His throne, "high and lifted up." And what was recorded next? The prophet declares that *"the train of His robe filled the temple."* The "train" was the hemmed portion or the back end of a king's robe. This train would signify the extent of that king's authority and power. As kings and their nations would conquer the other nations, the triumphant king would cut off a piece of the conquered king's robe and have that piece sewn into his train.

Therefore, the more victories that a king would have, the longer his train would be filled. Look at how the Bible described the "train" on the Lord's robe; "It filled the temple." Now let's remain mindful that today we are God's temples. The temple that He is now filling is not an external building, but rather it is the very essence of our beings. Just like in Isaiah's vision, today God is still looking for His train to fill our temples.

God by way of His Spirit has filled you with the fullness of His victory. He has filled your life with the fullness of His power and authority. No longer shall our lives reflect ones of defeat and misery. No longer shall God's people reflect an empty and deserted temple.

One meaning of the concept of being filled is to be "fully furnished." God wants His temples today to be "fully furnished" with His presence with no vacancies. We shall be the image of a temple that is now the dwelling place of a victorious, and all powerful God. It is with our lives that others shall also see God "high and lifted up" with all of His victory and glory filling our temples. This here, my friends, is what it means to have God's Spirit living within you and filling your life with God's glory.

Being Baptized

> *"I indeed baptize you with water unto repentance, but He who is coming after me is mightier than I, whose sandals I am not worthy to carry. He will baptize you with the Holy Spirit and fire"* *(Matthew 3:11, NKJV).*

What an awesome promise that we have here. This word "baptized" is the Greek word "baptizo," which means to be "immersed." This carries the imagery of someone being dropped or dipped into some water from head to toe. Every inch and ounce of their body being immensely soaked in this water. It's being overwhelmed and submerged in the immersion of something. In this case, this immersion is of the Spirit of God.

Imagine jumping into the deep end of a swimming pool and having all of your body plunged under water. Once you come out of the pool, every part of your body would be soaked and wet with this water. There would be no part of you untouched or dry. Everywhere that you would go you would be drenched, dripping water and leaving puddles behind. No one would let you into their homes because of the water that would be following you. No one would have to question the experience that you just had with the pool. The evidence would be all on you!

This immersion is the intent and purpose of the baptism of the Holy Spirit. It is that you would be immersed, soaked, overwhelmed and drenched with the life, power, and grace of God. No one would be able to deny His presence and your encounter with Him because there would be undeniable evidence. The disciples would become so immersed in God's Spirit that even their shadows and handkerchiefs would heal people (Acts 5:15, 19:12). We should be immersed and led by God's Spirit within every area of our lives. Through this immersion, all of God's power is at your disposal for the purposes of His Kingdom.

It was said of Jesus that He had the *"spirit without measure"* (*John 3:34, NASB*). That is an unlimited measure of God's Spirit. We too have this privilege that has been extended to us as well by way of the baptism. Unlike Jesus, many of God's people are operating in a limited measure of God's power simply because we get to decide on how much of God we desire to experience.

> *"Measuring as he went, he took me along the stream for 1,750 feet and then led me across. The water was up to my ankles. He measured off another 1,750 feet and led me across again. This time, the water was up to my knees. After another 1,750 feet, it was up to my waist. Then he measured another 1,750 feet, and the river was too deep to walk across. It was deep enough to swim in, but too deep to walk through"* (Ezekiel 47:3-5, NLT).

The imagery of water was oftentimes a depiction of the outpouring of God's Spirit. This passage is a perfect illustration of this. Let's focus in on this water that had just begun to exit the temple. At first, this water begins at this person's ankles. Then to their knees. Soon the water would be waist high. Eventually, this water would be too high and "too deep" for them to walk in. He would need to swim through this water.

Too many times we have become comfortable walking in the shallow end of God's presence. We will quickly settle for an ankle deep anointing. Some may even go further with God and desire a knee deep measure of His presence. If we are to live a distinguished life, we must begin to desire within our hearts a measure of His presence that is too much to walk in.

We need the immersion of His Spirit to overtake us. If there were ever a river to find yourself getting lost in, this would be that river. The very river of God's presence and anointing. It is only after the river was too high to walk in that it began to flow and bring life to everything that it touched. Let's become immersed in His Spirit so that life may begin to flow from us as well! Living a distinguished life is seen as we begin to carry the presence of God everywhere we go. Be mindful that you will never be able to carry something that you haven't first become immersed in for yourself!

I remember that night like it was yesterday. My wife, who was at the time my fiancée, led me to my experience of being filled by God. She first explained to me that if I were to ask God for the gift of the Holy Spirit, He would not give me something that would be detrimental for my life (Luke 11:13). She explained to me that being baptized in God's Spirit wasn't something that I should be afraid of either. Instead, it was to be a life-changing encounter that would revolutionize every area of my life. She then began to explain what is known as "speaking in tongues," or having a "Heavenly language." She was building my expectation of what was to come.

Eventually, after trying to talk myself out of this unknown experience, I began to encounter God's sweet presence. Then I began to utter unknown syllables. This utterance would serve as one sense of evidence of becoming filled with God's Spirit. For one, I share my testimony because it doesn't at first appear to be as dramatic as I have seen and heard other accounts to be. I share this because not every experience of the baptism will be an extreme and intense moment.

There are many people whose encounters were much like mine. I knew that I was filled and baptized in God's Spirit that night. I can testify that with this baptism my whole life had changed. Nothing has been the same since. The same can be true for you. As you come to experience the fullness of God's Spirit, just know that life as you once knew it will never be the same either. God has greater in store for you, and it all begins with an encounter with the Holy Spirit.

Someone may ask, "Why wouldn't everyone want to be immersed in God's Spirit?" One reason would be due to the spirituality of the person who desires to be acquainted with God's Spirit. Our natural minds will never allow us to receive something or in this case someone that our natural reasoning cannot comprehend. Becoming immersed and filled with God's Spirit doesn't make sense to the natural mind. In a society where intellectualism is esteemed, encounters with an invisible God seems illogical. Therefore, one reason why so many people miss out on this life altering moment is simply that they are not able to wrap their minds around this experience.

Let me encourage you today. This encounter isn't something that you gather brochures on and watch YouTube clips on until you have finally figured it out. It is to be an experience that is first led with your heart even when you can't understand it with your mind. Remember, that it is the all-wise and all-knowing God who uses the *"foolish things of the world to confound the wise" (1 Corinthians 1:27, KJV).*

It was the first-century church who had no manuals, teachings, literature or videos on this new phenomenon called the baptism. They would first encounter God's Spirit; then they would be taught about this new experience. Perhaps this may be the approach that God wants to take with you. Perhaps He's been after your heart so that your mind will no longer get in the way of an experience that will change the courses of your life. I challenge you to no longer think your way out of a true experience with God's Spirit. Instead, allow yourself to relinquish your heart and your life to God so that all that you are may be filled with all that He is.

Another reason why so many people remain reserved with this encounter is out of fear. Fear of the unknown. What is going to happen to me during this encounter? Will I still be able to have control of my life from this point forward? Will I begin to walk around looking weird like that lady or man at church? If the truth is told, these are all some legitimate questions that many of God's people have asked before.

Due to how many people have displayed what a Spirit filled life looks like, there has been much anxiety about the Holy Spirit. For instance, when I was coming up in the church I would see people "catching the Holy Ghost." In "catching the Holy Ghost," I would see these individuals sporadically begin to shout, dance and jump around. To be completely honest this "catching the Holy Ghost" just made them look weird and it made people like me scared. I didn't want anything to do with this Holy Ghost if this was what He made people do.

For the record, the Holy Spirit isn't a dance, a sporadic shout, or some random off the wall reaction. Never would I ever question the authenticity of someone's encounter with God, but I have come to the conclusion that these moments are not the Holy Spirit. They may be our responses and reactions to the Holy Spirit, but these moments in themselves are not Him.

In fact, we have attributed more religious moments in a church service to Him than we have the very power of God or His character. Never let someone else's responses or experiences deter you from a personal encounter with God. Remember, that it is the Holy Spirit who is referenced as the "good gift." The gift that your Heavenly Father will gladly give to you when you ask of Him.

> *"Don't be drunk with wine, because that will ruin your life. Instead, be filled with the Holy Spirit" (Ephesians 5:18, NKJV).*

I do want to expound on the concept of continuously being filled. There may be only one encounter in which you will become immersed in God's Spirit. It is also of God that we shall continue to be filled more and more throughout our lives with the Lord. Paul explains to us an amazing revelation about being filled with God's Spirit. In the original language of this passage it reads more like this; *"be being filled with the Holy Spirit."* Implying that we are not just to live the rest of our lives off of the initial encounter with the Holy Spirit, but that for the rest of our lives we shall expect to be continuously filled by God.

Imagine the cup of tea or lemonade that the waiter or waitress initially brought out to you while you were eating at your favorite restaurant. Once they had witnessed that your cup was low, they would take it upon themselves to give you a refill. In no way would they expect for you to enjoy your whole meal just off of the one glass of lemonade. They are well aware that throughout your stay you will need another refill. The interesting thing about this illustration is that a good waiter doesn't wait until your cup is almost empty before they offer the refill.

The same is true with God. He is well aware that as you aspire to a life of greatness, you too will be in need of a refill of God's Spirit. Just as your mobile phone needs to be rested, connected, and charged at the end of a long day, so do we as God's people. Living a distinguished life isn't just about a one-time encounter with God. It is about being in a constant relationship with God so that He may continue to grant you an even greater measure of His presence.

The Encounter That Leads To Purpose

Throughout the Bible, before God's people were used to fulfill their purposes for God, they first had an encounter with the Holy Spirit. Many people in the Old Testament experienced the Holy Spirit descending upon them before they would move forward with the plans of God. Even the apostles had to be filled first with the Holy Spirit before they were used by God to "turn the world upside down." If we desire to be world changers, we must first encounter God's presence. Being filled with God's Spirit will always be a prerequisite to our purpose.

Before Joshua was used by God to lead the Israelites into their promised land, he had to first be *"filled with the Spirit of wisdom"* (*Deuteronomy 34:9, NKJV*). Before Gideon was used to redeem God's people from their oppressors, he also had to experience the Spirit of God. *"Then the Spirit of the Lord clothed Gideon with power"* (*Judges 6:34, NLT*). Even our Lord and Savior had this encounter as the *"Spirit of God descended upon Him like a dove"* (*Matthew 3:16, NKJV*). Jesus and these others are the true epitome of living a distinguished life.

If we desire to live a life of purpose, being immersed and led by God's Spirit will always be a prerequisite. In fact, what qualifies and empowers us to be world changers are these experiences. We should never attempt to answer the amazing call of God for our lives in our own strength. Many times, I have even found myself chasing after purpose more than chasing after God's presence. One is the result of the other. And the criterion to walking into our God-given purposes is first to be led by His Spirit.

The Father's Promise, Not His Option

Let's set this next scene up. Jesus had just laid down His life on the Cross, and His body has now come up missing from a tomb in which He was laid. The disciples are scratching their heads trying to figure out what to do. Perhaps, they were asking themselves, "Should we hide from those who just crucified our Lord?" "Should we go back to the life that we once knew before?" Maybe one of them had asked the others, "Should we try to carry out the plans that Jesus had been preparing us for?" We do not know if any of these were legitimate thoughts or questions amongst the disciples. We do know that Jesus did eventually appear to them with proof of His resurrection.

> *"And being assembled together with them, He commanded them not to depart from Jerusalem, but to wait for the Promise of the Father, "which," He said, "you have heard from Me; for John truly baptized with water, but you shall be baptized with the Holy Spirit not many days from now" (Acts 1:4-5, NKJV).*

His next set of instructions would set things into motion on how we will be able to fulfill our destinies in the Lord. When we consider God's plans for our lives, we tend to start to look up the closest seminaries, and ministry in training programs to attend. If we look carefully at this text, we see that none of these great suggestions were Jesus' instructions. He simply instructs them to not "depart from Jerusalem," but instead to wait for the "Promise of the Father." What was this "Promise of the Father" you may ask? Jesus tells them that for them to carry out His plans they had to first be "baptized with the Holy Spirit."

This baptism of God's Spirit was the "Father's Promise" to His followers. It was the fulfillment of this one "Promise" that positioned them to fulfill all of God's other promises for their lives. This instruction from Jesus wasn't a great idea or a suggestion, but it was God's plan "A" strategy to change the world. If we desire to change the world as they did, we must come to realize that the baptism of the Holy Spirit is the "Father's Promise" to us as well. When we fail to understand this, what was always designed to be the "Father's Promise" will become just another option in attempting to live a fulfilled life.

It has always been God's desire for all of His people to be filled with Himself. This "Promise" of being filled with God wasn't solely for the ministers, pastors, and the apostles. Learning to live apart from this "Promise" of the fullness of God is not learning to live at all. I couldn't imagine what living life would look like for me without being filled with Him. It is sad to see that we perceive this baptism and immersion as an option and not a prerequisite for purposeful living.

There is a story of the tribes of Reuben, Gad, and half of Manasseh, deciding to no longer wait for the promise land (Numbers 32). Rather, they decided to settle on the east side of the Jordan River. They decided to settle for another option and not the promise. If you were to read this story, notice that God didn't argue with them. Instead, He let them settle for what they wanted. This mindset to settle for less than God's promises is true today. Today's promise land is no longer tied to a place, but rather a presence. The fullness of God's promise is now by way of His Spirit.

As it was with these tribes, so it is also with us today. A great portion of God's people is deciding to settle apart from this "Promise" of being baptized in God's Spirit. There are too many of us attempting to use other methods to achieve greatness. When we have decided to settle apart from the immersion of God's Spirit, we have also decided to settle with living less than a distinguished life. All of the promises of God are brought to fruition by first being filled with the "Promise of the Father." If we truly love God with all of our hearts, let's no longer settle for not being filled with the One that we love. Let's go all the way with God. Let's become immersed and filled with the Holy Spirit of God.

The River of God

Perhaps I have enticed you and stirred up your curiosity about God's Spirit. That will be awesome if that is the case. Let's take a look at what life would look like if we were all filled with God's presence. Let's see how we could all impact our communities for the Kingdom of God. Let's go back to the account of Ezekiel's river.

"In my vision, the man brought me back to the entrance of the Temple. There I saw a stream flowing east from beneath the door of the Temple and passing to the right of the altar on its south side. The man brought me outside the wall through the north gateway and led me around to the eastern entrance. There I could see the water flowing out through the south side of the east gateway" (Ezekiel 47:1-2, NLT).

The water of this river is a picture of the flowing grace and anointing of God in the lives of His people. This water is a prophetic picture of the outpouring of His Spirit. We must pay attention to the fact that the water was flowing away from the temple, not to the temple. The Kingdom of God is not about getting people to our buildings and churches. It is about getting the church to leave the buildings and go out to the people. The further the water went away from the temple, the deeper it got, and the more powerful was its impact. The same will be true with us as we learn to yield to the river of the Holy Spirit within our lives.

Jesus told His disciples that from you shall *"flow rivers of living water" (John 7:38, NKJV)*. If we desire to see the River of God flow through us, the first thing that we must be willing to do is to allow this river to overtake us. I stated earlier; you cannot carry something that you have not become immersed in first for yourself. It is as we willfully yield our lives to Him that we will find this river flowing from us.

"Then he said to me, "This river flows east through the desert into the valley of the Dead Sea. The waters of this stream will make the salty waters of the Dead Sea fresh and pure. There will be swarms of living things wherever the water of this river flows. Fish will abound in the Dead Sea, for its waters will become fresh. Life will flourish wherever this water flows" (Ezekiel 47:8-9, NLT).

This river was able to turn even the most polluted water into fresh and pure water, and it brought an abundance of life to wherever it went. Ezekiel says that the "fish will abound" for the "waters will become fresh." Be mindful that Jesus did tell His disciples that he would make them "fishers of men." Could this promise of the abundance of souls be fulfilled as God's Spirit and river flows through our lives? I'd like to imagine so. As God's Spirit fills our lives, He will use us to bring freshness and purity to even the most impoverished places in the world.

I once remember reading of the accounts and stories of the Welsh revival in 1904-1905, in which there was a revival in the nation of Wales. It was said that many of the bars, clubs, and jail cells were empty. Crime came to a complete stop. All of their sports events and season were abruptly canceled. The nation's economy was revived. Homes, marriages, and families were restored. The entire nation was changed and radically impacted. This transformation came without all of the various strategies that we use today to bring about practical changes.

There were no political agendas, parties or elections needed for this change. There was no need for any church campaigns or conferences. No bailouts, marches, protests or rallies were used. Just simply an outpouring of God's Spirit upon the willing hearts and repentant lives. Wherever God's Spirit flowed throughout this nation transformation took place. An entire country was impacted simply because God's Spirit showed up!

> *"Life will flourish wherever this water flows"* (Ezekiel 47:9, NLT).
> *"The water that I shall give him will become in him a fountain of water springing up into everlasting life"* (John 4:14, NKJV).

It is this river and outpouring of the Holy Spirit that brings life. It has always been that God's people would serve as the conduit of this river. In every aspect of our society, there is a desperate need for this new life. Instead of God's people always being the ones who need this life the most, we should be the ones that God causes this new life to flow from to others.

His Power and Anointing

"But you shall receive power when the Holy Spirit has come upon you." (Acts 1:8, NKJV). One thing that the Holy Spirit should be synonymous with is power. Not just any power that we may have been exposed to before. This power is the true, unlimited, life changing, Kingdom building power that only comes from the living God. The significance of a disciple's life is that being an inferior, weak being, an almighty God has decided to fill our lives with His power.

"But if the Spirit of Him who raised Jesus from the dead dwells in you, He who raised Christ from the dead will also give life to your mortal bodies through His Spirit who dwells in you" (Romans 8:11, NKJV).

The great news for us is that the same Holy Spirit that raised Jesus up is alive within us. He desires to use that same resurrection, life-giving power in our lives as well! So that we may be effective witnesses of God, He has given us this power. We are the power lines, and God's power is the current of electricity that is transferred through our lives. To ensure that God truly empowers us, He has placed His all-powerful presence within us.

"But the manifestation of the Spirit is given to each one for the profit of all" (1 Corinthians 12:7, NKJV).

Look at what Paul references these gift of God as; the "manifestation of the Spirit." All the spiritual gifts of God that are in your life are just the manifestations of God's Spirit. If these gifts are manifestations of God's presence in your life, seek Him about how He wants to manifest these gifts. Please do not limit how God has determined for His power and presence to manifest through you. It is His gifts, miracles, and power that are simply the manifestation of His Spirit.

Partnering With The Holy Spirit

Lastly, so that we may live distinguished lives in the Lord, it is not always a matter of needing more power from God in our lives. Rather, we may need to learn how to partner with the Holy Spirit. Where there has been a lack of results in our churches, services, or communities, we begin to pray for more power. Sometimes, the strategy of God is that we come to learn the importance of partnering with the power that we already have.

Being a major sports fan, I have seen this play out so many times within sports. One team may be more athletic, faster, stronger and bigger. They may have even loaded up with the top athletes just so that they may dominate their opponents. Even with all of their talent, if they have not become a cohesive unit, then this lack of partnering can become their demise. It is only a matter of time before they fall victim to a team that can effectively work and partner together to bring about their defeat.

> *"May the grace of the Lord Jesus Christ, the love of God, and the fellowship of the Holy Spirit be with you all" (2 Corinthians 13:14, NLT).*

Often, we focus on God's power and not a fellowship with Him. To fellowship with God is to partner with Him. It is to co-labor with God pertaining to His plans and purposes. To have this "fellowship with the Holy Spirit" is to learn the personality and presence of God. It is as we partner with God that we begin to experience the power of God.

The Holy Spirit is a person as much as we are. He has emotions, feelings, thoughts, plans and strategies. Trust me; His ways are so much better than ours. Imagine the difference between your "OnStar" assistance versus the GPS navigational system in your vehicle. Your GPS is a programmed satellite system that is designed to assist you as you tell it where you are looking to go. Although the operator may have a voice that comes on to assist you, this operating system has no personality.

While on the other hand, the operator with your "OnStar" service is a real, live agent who has thoughts, feelings, and emotions. This agent is one button away from assisting you in your times of need. Unlike the "OnStar" system, the Holy Spirit is closer than one button away; He is in you. He has a personality that we must become accustomed to if we ever desire to partner with God. It is pivotal that we come to learn how He operates, how He thinks, and How He desires to move in you.

"Can two walk together, unless they are agreed?" (Amos 3:3, NKJV). This passage has as much of a meaning when it comes to our relationships with God, as it does with His people. To effectively partner with God's Spirit, we must learn to agree with Him concerning His will. Yes, power is necessary. Learning to partner with His power is necessary as well.

This partnership doesn't happen overnight. It takes the time to learn how to hear His voice and learn of His ways. Even in your most modest attempts, you are going to miss what He's doing, but God is kind and patient concerning His people. Don't beat up on yourself if this is ever the case, and trust me at times it will be. Just as a baby learns to walk, you will find yourself gradually learning to walk alongside God's Spirit and partner with Him in His work.

This new life of power and partnering takes having a true relationship with God. Not for the sake of what He can do for you, but solely for who He is and what He has done for you through Jesus. God wants to use us, not for us to use Him! A distinguished life is first having a relinquished life before the Holy Spirit.

A life of purpose is one where we have allowed the world to see what the life of Jesus truly looks like in our lives. There is someone around you that is waiting for God's presence and light to begin to illuminate and shine through you. Become a carrier of His presence. Become one who God can use to change the world for His Kingdom. And let's begin to live distinguished by first becoming immersed in His Spirit.

This is a chapter that was not to be just read, but to be experienced. Perhaps your heart is now at a place to experience more of God's Spirit in a new and greater way. If this is the case, I would like to encourage you to make this prayer personal for yourself:

God, I thank you for placing your Spirit within me. This day I desire to experience more of your presence within my life. Father, I ask that you will baptize me with your Spirit. Fill me to overflow with your presence. Immerse me in your anointing, and take me deeper into your love. Holy Spirit, cause your rivers to flow over me, in me, and through me. Stir up your gifts in me, and display your power in my life. Grant me the evidence of being filled with your presence now. I ask that you will continue to live your life within me in Jesus' name, Amen!

5

Distinguished By The Mind of Christ

n 2011 my wife and I went to see what would become one of my absolute favorite movies of all time called "Limitless." In this movie, a man played by Bradley Cooper would be what today's society has deemed as a loser. He lived in a filthy, dislodged apartment. He didn't have a job. As an aspiring writer, he suffered from a major case of writer's block. To the point that he could never get beyond the first couple of pages of his book. His girlfriend would end up leaving him because he seemed to be stuck in life. It was safe to say that this man didn't have much in life going for himself, until one day he comes across a little clear pill that would radically change his life forever.

This pill would give him access to 100% of his brain and its functionality. Therefore, instantly he was able to think clearly, and see life with all of its potentials. He would learn to capitalize on all of life's opportunities for success and greatness. The book that he was never able to begin writing he finished in a matter of a few days. He became a stockbroker and became wealthy overnight. He learned foreign languages in a matter of hours and would end up being adored by some of the biggest personalities in town. It would be an understatement to say that this small little clear pill brought significance to his life all in a matter of days. This pill distinguished him!

As my wife and I were leaving the theater, I began to ponder what life would be like if one had that much access to his/her brains. How would life be different? What measures of success could one have? As clearly as someone speaking directly to you, the Lord spoke the following words that would change how I would see life forever. God's Spirit spoke gently to me and said, *"And you do not even need a pill."* Immediately, a passage came to my mind that served as confirmation that what I heard was from God. *"But we have the mind of Christ"* (1 Corinthians 2:16, NKJV).

Wow! How amazing is that? It will not be a special pill that will cause us to live a quality of life that only Hollywood could portray. It is with the mind of Christ that we can dream dreams. With James Cameron, it was said that he had to wait over a decade for technology to be created and catch up to the vision that he had for his box office hit "Avatar." Imagine having a measure of vision from God that would exceed the technology that exists in our modern day times. Or to come up with the next multi-million and billion-dollar idea that will revolutionize how the world is to live, exist and operate.

Contrary to the movie "Limitless," this truth is not about having 100% access to our minds, but instead, it is having access to His mind. Why would we want more access to our finite and limited minds, when He has invited us to have access to His infinite mind and wisdom? The creator of the universe and the One, who placed the stars in the sky has invited us to think like Him, see life like Him, and live like Him by having His mind. Now this, ladies and gentlemen, is what I would call living distinguished.

By His Spirit

The invitation and the ability to have the mind of Christ is not a result of a pill, formula or philosophy. It is the result of being led by God's Spirit. The mind of Christ becomes a reality in our lives when we allow our thoughts to become like God's thoughts. It is by God's Spirit that we will be able to receive the creative thoughts and clever ideas from God.

> *"But as it is written: "Eye has not seen, nor ear heard, Nor have entered into the heart of man The things which God has prepared for those who love Him." But God has revealed them to us through*

His Spirit. For the Spirit searches all things, yes, the deep things of God" (1 Corinthians 2:9-10, NKJV).

Consider what Paul says first, *"Eye has not seen, nor ear heard, Nor have entered into the heart of man the things which God has prepared for those who love Him."* Begin to imagine that there are great things that God has planned for your life. Eyes have not seen what God has in store for you. Ears have never heard the world-changing strategies that await God's people. It has never "entered into the hearts of men" the great things that God has destined to use their lives to bring into existence.

If you have caught onto this invitation within your heart, then it is only right that you would ask, "How do I get to the mind of Christ?" I'm glad that you asked! If we continue with the passage that has been referenced above, we will find the answer to our question. *"But God has revealed them to us through His Spirit. For the Spirit searches all things, yes the deep things of God."* This invitation to having the mind of Christ is only revealed through God's Spirit. It is the Holy Spirit that brings us to a place where we can first be receptive to the ways and truths of God. It is also the Holy Spirit who will cause us to think and see as God.

Joseph in the Bible is a great example of what it looks like to the mind of Christ. As Pharaoh would share his dream with Joseph, he begins to not only interpret it, but he also begins to provide a God-given strategy. It is when we have the mind of Christ that we will be able to interpret dreams, and provide strategies to the kings of this world. Imagine seeing the world coming to God's people for the answers and plans for some of the world's biggest issues. Imagine how the Glory of God would be revealed in a practical everyday way in this world.

> *"So Pharaoh asked his officials, "Can we find anyone else like this man so obviously filled with the spirit of God?" Then Pharaoh said to Joseph, "Since God has revealed the meaning of the dreams to you, clearly no one else is as intelligent or wise as you are" (Gen 41:38-39, NLT).*

Did you catch that? Pharaoh attributed Joseph's intelligence, discernment and interpretations to the fact that God's Spirit was with him. It is evident that there's a degree of wisdom that can only come from God. The same Spirit that was responsible for using Joseph in an amazing way also desires to use you.

The Natural Mind

Perhaps you may be asking yourself, "How come we all don't experience this mind of Christ?" This question would be a logical question with a very logical and simple answer. As saved as we may be in the Lord, we still have a natural mindset. When I say that we all have a "natural mindset," I'm not referring to an everyday logical reasoning that is necessary to live and be productive. I'm talking about the theory and philosophies of life that serve as a contradiction to the truths and ways of God.

> *"These things we also speak, not in words which man's wisdom teaches but which the Holy Spirit teaches, comparing spiritual things with spiritual. But the natural man does not receive the things of the Spirit of God, for they are foolishness to him; nor can he know them, because they are spiritually discerned" (1 Corinthians 2:13-14, NKJV).*

Paul defines what I call a "natural mindset" as "man's wisdom." It's this wisdom of man that influences us to continue to think more like the world and less like God. It's the "natural mindset" that struggles to receive God's truths and keeps us out of the loop with what God is doing all around us. If the Kingdom of God was a team, and Jesus was the coach, then God's word is our playbook. We will never be able to run the plays of God successfully without knowing His playbook, and having His mind. It's the natural mindset that can hinder us from thinking like God. There are a few other factors that prevent many people from experiencing a distinguished life and having the mind of Christ.

Strongholds

> *"For though we walk in the flesh, we do not war according to the flesh. For the weapons of our warfare are not carnal but mighty in God for pulling down strongholds, casting down arguments and every high thing that exalts itself against the knowledge of God, bringing every thought into captivity to the obedience of Christ, and being*

ready to punish all disobedience when your obedience is fulfilled" (2 Corinthians 10:3-6, NKJV).

It would be safe to say that every believer has dealt with what Paul refers to as a stronghold. A stronghold is anything that someone believes, places their trust in and relies on to live and exist. It is any concept or way of thinking that one has come to depend on over the ways and truths of God.

Therefore, it gives the enemy and his lies access within your life. The enemy would love nothing more than to hinder you from experiencing all that Jesus' death has fulfilled. As a disciple of Jesus, your life may belong to God, but too many times our minds and thoughts are up for grabs. This enemy knows that your mind is the driver's seat to your life, and it's your thoughts that steer your life in the directions that you will go.

We all have come to Christ with presupposed mindsets and dependencies that were opposing the ways of God. Without these mindsets being transformed by God's word, we will continue to go on with life frustrated and wondering why God isn't working in our lives. Historically, a stronghold was a particular place in which a certain kingdom would build high walls to protect its fortresses. This form of protection would keep these kingdoms safe within and keep the intruders out. This image would be an accurate picture of how Satan uses these mental strongholds in the lives of people today.

With all of the various ways of thinking that we came to Christ with, we tend to place forms of protection around these ways of thinking. Just like the strongholds in the ancient days of civilization, we have mental walls that we have put up that will keep us from receiving Gods truths. These walls have kept us from experiencing the true freedom that we have in Christ. These walls also protect and keep the lies of the enemy from being addressed and replaced with God's truths.

A stronghold is any philosophy that we hold to a higher regard than the truths of God. It is interesting to know that every day we think thousands upon thousands of thoughts. Imagine how many of these thoughts go unchecked and unchallenged by God's word. These thoughts then have a chance to be eventually exalted above the truths of God.

Oftentimes, we are very reluctant to have our natural theories to life challenged by God. It is as if we get comfortable in the darkness of the enemies lies and the shade that this world's philosophies have provided. We have shunned away any light of God's Gospel and the freedom that comes with His light. Therefore, we naturally establish strongholds that protect these wrong ways of thinking and lies so that we may continue to live comfortable in the midst of life's uncertainties.

When God goes to prepare His people for His blessings, He will ultimately have to deal with any mindset that opposes His truths. *"My people are destroyed for lack of knowledge" (Hosea 4:6, NKJV).* The enemy has always fed on the ignorance of God's people, and he will always take advantage of what we do not know. The enemy cannot stop God's people nor prevent us from fulfilling our destinies. However, he can influence us to stop ourselves. This has been done primarily by getting us to believe and come into agreement with his lies.

We often blame the enemy for our blessings being "held up." The majority of the time we are giving him too much credit and not taking enough responsibility for hindering God's blessings in our own lives. It's having the wrong mindset that limits the blessings of God more than anything else. We must take ownership of the lies we have accepted and the areas that we have remained ignorant to the ways of God.

Warfare

Warfare and strongholds go hand in hand. The strongholds of the enemy may at times be a result of us succumbing to the attacks of the enemy. In fact, the enemy often engages warfare in the areas where we struggle with believing God's truths. Warfare could be defined as the series of attacks, strategies, and plans that the enemy will attempt to do in the life of a believer. These attacks are with the intentions to thwart the plans of God within our lives and to get us to forfeit the victory of God.

We all have experienced bad days where we may have had a flat tire on the way to work. Or that nagging co-worker continued to work our last nerve. Or we may have even experienced a physical illness right before a major breakthrough. I would never put these examples and circumstances past the enemy to try to slow God's people down.

The ultimate battlefield is in our minds. Even the physical ailments are all designed to bring you mentally down to a discouraged place. The enemy knows that where the head is the body will follow. If he can get to our minds through his continuous attacks, then he will hinder God's plans for our lives.

One of the common goals of the enemy's attacks upon the minds of people is to cause mental confusion and distractions. Sometimes the warfare on our minds may present themselves as cloudiness in our thoughts, a lack of clarity in our thinking, anxiety, and confusion in our minds. When confused and cloudy in our thought life we are much more prone to make irrational decisions, compromise our convictions and remain ignorant to the ways of God.

Like a cornerback who is covering a wide receiver, they cannot cause the receiver not to catch the ball through physical contact. This physical contact would be considered a pass interference. They can become such a nuisance that they may distract the receiver and make it difficult for him. This form of distraction is how the enemy works in our lives as well. He cannot stop God's promises for your life. He can only attempt to distract you and make it difficult for you.

Distractions and confusion against the mind have been one of his greatest weapons. With having the mind of Christ, we can navigate around the enemy's distractions and move forward in the things of God. Be encouraged that in Christ we are "more than conquerors!" Our fight is fixed, and our battle is against a defeated foe. Satan's strategies are like someone playing checkers, while the strategies in having the mind of Christ is like playing chess. The King still has one more move; checkmate!

Cleansed Conscience

> *"And since we have a great High Priest who rules over God's house, let us go right into the presence of God with sincere hearts fully trusting him. For our guilty consciences have been sprinkled with Christ's blood to make us clean, and our bodies have been washed with pure water" (Hebrews 10:21-22, NLT).*

For many of us, when we get our cars washed, we tend to have that clean car feeling. We may actually feel a little different with having a clean car as opposed to driving it when it is dirty. I know that this is normally the case for most people. Having a cleansed car makes most of us feel different, and I bet a cleansed conscience will have the same effect.

It is a sinful, guilty conscience that entangles many of God's people. Many people have cried out asking, "if I am saved, then why do I still feel like I want to keep sinning?" Another thought may be, "no matter how hard I try, I can't seem to break these sinful habits." It's a sinful and guilty conscience that will also hinder us from experiencing the freedom in Jesus. It's the sinful conscience that continues to cause us to naturally bend towards our old sinful habits. These habits do not arise back into our lives because there is some part of our salvation that we missed. It is simply because where there's a mindset that has not been renewed, and there are still strongholds that exist.

This conscience causes us to remain aware of our wrongs and sins more than the works of Jesus. With this mindset, we tend to be more reluctant to approach God when we mess up. We tend to hold ourselves hostage to the mistakes and decisions that we have made. If God is not condemning us, then we should not allow the enemy to do so either. It was the shed blood of Jesus that delivered us from our old sinful and guilty conscience. We are now invited to have a cleansed conscience in the Lord.

A cleansed conscience is where we are mindful and persuaded in the works of God more than our failures and sins. I hear so many people praying for the deliverance from many sins. I wonder how many of those sins and their influences would be of no effect if we recognized the cleansed conscience that we now have with the mind of Christ? What habits of ours can only be broken with a cleansed conscience? What if we all would truly receive the revelations of God's love and redemption? I'd bet we would walk around differently and live differently like those who drive with that clean car feeling.

Not only does the blood cleanse our conscience from sin, its guilt, and its influences, but it also cleanses our hearts and minds from the effects of sin. Such as sickness, mental illness, depression, fear, perversion, confusion, etc. These things are not the root of sin; instead, they are the results of sin. It was His blood that cleansed us from all of the ailments of sin and a fallen world.

Many doctors believe that all sicknesses are "psychosomatic." This is when the physical illnesses would originate from the thoughts of our hearts and mind (conscience). It's our condemning, unforgiving, and shameful thoughts that may cause the physical issues within our bodies. It is this bondage of unforgiveness, shame, and resentment that may be the open door to many physical and mental ailments. The cells within our bodies are just responding to the issues within our hearts (Proverbs 4:23).

These are issues that only the Gospel can truly heal. What if the true healing agent in this world wasn't the counseling sessions, medicines, and fitness plans? What if it was the blood of Jesus that washes away our sins and causes us to have a cleansed conscience? What things have you been entangled with that only a cleansed conscience by the blood of Jesus can deliver you from? For those living a distinguished life, a cleansed conscience is crucial to everyday living. We must be mindful that it is not something that we are asking God to do, but it is a realization of what He has already done. Take a moment and thank God for the blood of Jesus that has given you a cleansed conscience.

A Victorious Mindset

Everyone wants a victorious mindset. Few people have come to realize that victory is a mindset. Victory begins with one's receptivity and belief in the finished works of Jesus. To have the mind of Christ is to have a victorious mindset. Not a mindset that causes you to waiver back and forth in your faith. Without understanding the finished works of Jesus, it will become inevitable that we will live a frustrated and defeated life.

Having a victorious mindset recognizes that we are to start off our day and go on to our jobs with the victory, not looking to gain victory. It's not getting the promotion on your job that makes you victorious; it is having victory before the promotion. Knowing this will always position you for true elevation. It's not winning the awards, having accomplishments and achievements that define your success. It is learning to live from what Jesus has already accomplished that shall define your success. We are to experience the mind of Christ as we come to embrace what I would like to call God's "3 R's;" repentance, renewed mind, and revelation.

Repentance

For a moment, let's say that you were driving from Nashville, TN to a certain vacation destination in Florida. After a few hours of driving, you find yourself crossing the Arkansas state line. It wouldn't take you long to realize that you will not be arriving in Florida anytime soon and that you were driving in the wrong direction. Immediately you would stop, turn around and begin to go in the right direction. This illustration would be an accurate example of true Biblical repentance. Repentance is actually a very encouraging concept when received correctly. It is one that is absolutely necessary in order to experience the mind of Christ.

It is so important that it was the first instruction that John the Baptist and Jesus both gave as they began their public ministries. *"From that time Jesus began to preach and to say, "Repent, for the kingdom of heaven is at hand" (Matthew 4:17, NKJV).* What was so important about this particular message? Jesus had now arrived on the scene, and He had come to usher in a new Kingdom. For the people to be able to experience the fullness of His Kingdom, repentance would be necessary.

Repentance means to change and turn from one way of thinking to change your way of living. It is to turn from going in the wrong directions in life so that we may go in the directions of life that God has destined for His people. To experience a distinguished life, we must be willing to turn from the ways of the world and turn to the ways of God. Repentance is to acknowledge where we have failed and sinned and to repent for these things. Repentance is not only to be forgiven but to be changed and transformed. Transformation is the aim.

Bill Johnson said in his book *"Heaven Invades Earth," "Most Christians repent enough to get forgiven, but not enough to see the Kingdom"* (pg. 37). In other words, we repent so that we can have peace that God has forgiven our sins. Still, we miss the true reason for repentance. Repentance is not just an act that we do when we have sinned. It is to be a lifestyle that we have learned to implement so that we may be active participants in God's Kingdom. Repentance would be the first "R." Our second one would be what Paul calls the "renewing of our minds."

The Renewed Mind

> *"And do not be conformed to this world, but be transformed by the renewing of your mind, that you may prove what is that good and acceptable and perfect will of God" (Romans 12:2, NKJV).*

This passage has always been one of my favorite passages in the entire Bible. Paul is urging the church in Rome not to remain accustomed to the traditions and ways of the world. Instead, he admonishes them to learn to welcome the transformed life that comes by way of having a renewed mind. This word "renew" means to bring something to a "complete change for the better." Wow, think about that!

This is God's plan for you. To have the mind of Christ, the Holy Spirit must bring about a "complete change" of our minds.

This renewal of the mind is a result of God drawing us into His word and teaching us His ways. He causes our thoughts and our minds to begin to comprehend His principles and precepts. By the renewing of our minds, God begins to bring our thoughts and our lives into a perfect alignment with His word. It is also having a renewed mind that causes us to have the mind of Christ.

We cannot expect Kingdom blessings with a worldly mindset. We cannot expect God to bring about His Kingdom blessings according to the world's way of doing things. We will always miss out on God's plans. The challenge is not to be so consumed with our own natural surroundings that we could miss how God is moving within our lives. When God wants to bless someone He will oftentimes have to bring them to a renewed mind or else they may hold up His blessings.

I remember a time when I kept receiving alerts on my smartphone that it was ready for a software update. I chose to ignore these alerts continuously. That was until my phone began to malfunction. My phone was trying to communicate to me that there was a new operating system which needed to be downloaded. My phone was being invited to operate in a new way. For this to happen, I needed to allow the software update to take place. Only then could my phone function the way that it was truly intended to do.

The same could be said of us and God's plans for our lives. There are things that God desires to do with us, but if we do not embrace His software updates (renewed minds), then our lives can become stagnated. There are times when God needs to renew a certain train of thought in our minds in order to position us for His promises. We only come to experience these promises through a renewed mind. We cannot expect a new blessing with an old mindset. We cannot expect God's move in this season if we are still hanging onto last season's strategies.

What does a distinguished life look like? It looks like the ending portion of the mentioned verse above. *"That you may prove what is that good and acceptable and perfect will of God."* A distinguished life in the Lord is one that has been able to prove God's *"good and acceptable and perfect will."* Let's imagine what God's good, acceptable and perfect will is. It is God's will that you would have an abundant life, peace, healing, joy and wholeness. All of these things and so much more is God's perfect will for your life. We must come to realize that it is learning to have a renewed mind that gets us there. God wants to use your life to prove His awesome and good will, but a renewed mind is required for Him to do so.

Revelation

To conclude with the third component of our "3 R's," we must also be willing to receive God's divine revelation. Revelation can be defined as the unveiling of hidden truths or the revealing of concealed information. What this means is that God desires to reveal the secrets, truths and the strategies of Heaven to His people. To have revelation means to have been endowed by God with the secrets of the Kingdom. Paul referred to them as "mysteries."

> *"How that by revelation He made known to me the mystery (as I have briefly written already, by which, when you read, you may understand my knowledge in the mystery of Christ), which in other ages was not made known to the sons of men, as it has now been revealed by the Spirit" (Ephesians 3:3-5, NKJV).*

The truths of God's word are all around us today. Revelation is just the unveiling of God's truths that are right in front us. God is not in the business with His people playing the guessing game with their lives. The prophet Jeremiah once said that *"God knows the plans that He has for His people" (Jeremiah 29:11).* It is not enough that only He knows the plans for your life. God also wants you to know the plans for your life and to no longer be in the dark concerning them. It is by way of revelation that we begin to get the answers to life that only come from God. Revelation is when God turns the lights on within our lives and then we are finally able to see the truth for what it is.

> *"Live no longer as the Gentiles do, for they are hopelessly confused. Their minds are full of darkness; they wander far from the life God gives because they have closed their minds and hardened their hearts against him" (Ephesians 4:17-18, NLT).*

The Gentiles according to this verse were alienated from the *"life God gives"* because *"their minds are full of darkness."* To be restrained from God's revelation is to live in darkness. And to live in darkness is to have a mindset and understanding that has and is blinded from the truths of God. In the Bible, God's word has always been referred to as light. *"Your word is a lamp to my feet. And a light to my path."* *(Psalms 119:105, NKJV).* So that we may have the mind of Christ, we are in desperate need of God to turn on the lights and unveil His truths and revelations to us.

"And you will seek Me and find Me when you search for Me with all your heart." *(Jeremiah 29:13, NKJV)* How does one come to a place where they may receive God's revelations? It is as we begin to seek God with all of our hearts. To "seek" means to pursue passionately. When we begin to passionately seek and pursue God with all of our hearts, we will find ourselves in a place where His truths can be unveiled. It's like our hearts are the light switch. Whenever we allow God's hand to turn on the switch then can we come from the darkness of this world and function in the light of His revelation.

As God begins to ignite a hunger in our souls for more of Him, we will begin to pursue God radically through His word. *"It is the glory of God to conceal a matter, But the glory of kings is to search out a matter"* *(Proverbs 25:2, NKJV).* Why would God hide anything from His people? It is so that we would have to seek Him out for His truths. It's almost like God has placed the most precious valuables and jewels in His word. It is the hungry heart and renewed mind that is positioned to discover them!

Heavenly Minded

There has been an old saying which describes someone as "being so Heavenly minded that we are no earthly good." This means that someone has become so spiritual that they are no longer practical. Many people separate what's "spiritual" from what's "practical." I would like to suggest that if what's "spiritual" isn't "practical," then it isn't "spiritual" at all. To be "Heavenly minded," is to be earthly good in every sense of the term. In fact, I'd like to believe that this world needs more Heavenly minded people.

To be a Heavenly minded person is to be someone who sees this life, people, this world and all of its problems from a higher perspective. It is to see all things from a Heavenly perspective. This mindset isn't without still seeing the practicalities of this world and our everyday lives. Instead, it is to see everything that's around us as God does. Once again, this is what we have been invited to as we embrace the mind of Christ.

> *"Since you have been raised to new life with Christ, set your sights on the realities of heaven, where Christ sits in the place of honor at God's right hand. Think about the things of heaven, not the things of earth" (Colossians 3:1-2, NLT).*

Paul tells the church that they have been *"raised to new life with Christ."* Then Paul tells them how they are to experience this new life in the Lord; by setting their *"sights on the realities of Heaven."* I love this! This word "set" means to put or have something fixed in a certain and specific place. Paul is telling them to fix their focus on Heaven intentionally and to place their mindsets in the ways of God.

For many people, Heaven is only a fictional place that they will one day experience once they have died. To experience Heaven here and now is not a reality. This world has established and determined what reality is and what it is not. Our realities must begin to be reshaped and redefined by the ways of God and His word. This concept is the secret behind learning to be "Heavenly minded" and to set our minds on the realities of Heaven.

To be "Heavenly minded" is when we begin to understand the ways of the Kingdom and receive God's strategies for this world. Imagine being the one who would find the cure for AIDS and see cancer finally eradicated and defeated. It should be God's people, those who think like Him, who should formulate the plan to destroy poverty and world hunger. What are the problems of this world that are only designed to be fixed by those who have set their minds on the "realities of Heaven?" What problems of this world are waiting for someone to begin to think like God?

When your mind is focused on Heaven, so will your life also be. Healings may take place in our bodies, but wholeness and health begin in our minds. Healing isn't just a miracle; it's a mindset. Joy is not a season or circumstance. Joy is a mindset. Peace is a mindset. Victory is not contingent on some events or breakthrough but rather victory is a mindset. How do we become persuaded, influenced focused on the Lord? It's by thinking and focusing on the things of H' the ways of God.

The Power Of Focus

When it comes to having the mind of Christ, it is imperative that we come to acknowledge the law of focus. Whatever you set your focus and attention to, whether it be good or bad, you will attract towards yourself in life. In fact, the majority of what we are experiencing now is the result of how we have become focused on a certain matter. It is as if God created such a thing called the law of focus. The law of focus being whatever you have set your reality and affections towards you shall come to experience. This is a constant theme throughout the Bible.

> *"Now Jacob took for himself rods of green poplar and of the almond and chestnut trees, peeled white strips in them, and exposed the white which was in the rods. And the rods which he had peeled, he set before the flocks in the gutters, in the watering troughs where the flocks came to drink, so that they should conceive when they came to drink. So the flocks conceived before the rods, and the flocks brought forth streaked, speckled, and spotted" (Genesis 30:37-39, NKJV).*

In this story, we have Jacob promising to take the spotted sheep (inferior agriculture) while giving Laban the unblemished, sheep with no spots (superior agriculture). How does Jacob trick Laban? By taking the good sheep with no spots, placed a stripped and spotted rod before the watering troughs, and when the sheep would go to these troughs, they would begin to mate and conceive while looking upon the rods. It was as they set their focus on the spotted rods near the troughs that these sheep would begin to conceive spotted lambs. In essence, the sheep gave birth to what they had set their focus on. We will also begin to give birth to and experience what we have set our focus on in life as well. Whatever has your attention is what will begin to consume your life. You will always empower whatever you're focusing on!

If God is your focus, then you shall begin to experience His promises. If the bondages of this world are what you have focused on, then you will also begin to experience these things overpowering your life. One major mistake that many of have committed is to believe that we can overcome our strongholds, and issues pay more attention to them and exert all of our efforts in overcoming them. someone's thoughts are "if I keep my addiction at the forefront of my mind, then one day I will stop indulging in my addictions." "Or maybe I will go buy all of the books, attend all of the seminars, and find as many people to pray for me as possible; then I will experience a deliverance over my issues."

Even when you attempt to address your sins, issues, or addictions through various methods, what you may be doing is empowering these afflictions by continuing to set your focus on them. The more that you give thought to your circumstances, the more that you will empower them within your life. The key is not to ignore your situations, but rather it is to shift your focus from your problems over to God. It is when we set our focus and attention on the things of God that we will begin to see the issues of life lose its influence. Our strongholds and addiction will no longer overtake our lives as our thoughts, focus, and our minds are now set on God, and the finished works of His Son.

This can be seen when God dealt judgment on Israel by sending serpents to attack God's people. The people's cry to Moses was to pray that God would cause the snakes to go away, but instead this was God's response to Moses, *"Make a fiery serpent, and set it on a pole; and it shall be that everyone who is bitten, when he looks at it, shall live" (Numbers 21:8, NKJV)*. It was as the people looked on the pole, and no longer set their focus on the snakes that they were saved from the snakes. In this story, the snakes did not go away, but instead the snakes could no longer harm God's people as they set their focus on this pole. This "bronzed serpent" pole is an Old Testament type for the Cross of Jesus, and even today as we set our focus and affection on the Cross, the issues of this world will no longer harm us. Perhaps, your addictions, issues, problems and strongholds are waiting on you to stop centering your attention onto them and begin to center your thoughts on God.

This principle can be seen in how the Psalmist tells us that *"I will lift up my eyes to the hills—From whence comes my help?" (Psalms 121:1, NKJV)*. We can see this as Hebrews tells us to *"look unto Jesus, the author and finisher of our faith" (Hebrews 12:2, NKJV)*. This law of focus is evident as Proverbs tells us that *"For as he thinks in his heart, so is he" (Proverbs 23:7, NKJV)*. We can even see this truth put to practice as Peter walked on the water while focusing on Jesus, but then began to sink as he took his eyes off of Christ (Matthew 14:29). Living a distinguished life is seen as we begin to shift our attention from what is going on around us to Jesus, who is always before us. As our focus is on Christ, not only will we have the mind of Christ, but we will also begin to experience the fullness of God's blessings.

The Snake Line

There is a part of a mountain that is very high that is called "the snake line." The "snake line" is referencing a certain altitude on a mountain in which a snake is not able to breathe and survive. There is a principle that many have learned to apply in their lives as believers. That is that at a certain altitude spiritually, there are some issues that cannot survive. We should be mindful that God has called us to live from a high place in Him. A place where there are no snakes, sickness, poverty, depression and so on.

"And raised us up together, and made us sit together in the heavenly places in Christ Jesus" (Ephesians 2:6, NKJV). Where are we to be seated? That's right; we are seated with Christ in "heavenly places." What does that mean? It means that just as Jesus is now in Heaven seated at the right hand of God, so are we as we are in Him. Therefore, our existence, living, and thinking come from where we are seated; Heaven.

One may say, "This sounds ridiculous," and of course, it may take some time to truly comprehend. Yes, we live here on earth, but spiritually our mindset and our mentality derive from above. In fact, how we walk here on earth should always be a reflection of how we are seated in Heaven. Just as it is that snakes are not able to survive in a certain high altitude, I totally believe that all of the issues that have plagued this world are not able to exist in Heaven where we are seated with Christ.

We must come to embrace a higher mindset in the Lord. I have come to believe that to experience God's deliverance in every area of our lives; we must have a change of mind and heart. In fact, I don't believe that God is in the business of just delivering His people from snakes (sickness, depression, fear, etc.). Instead, God is in the business of calling us to come live above the snake line.

Oftentimes, we have become accustomed to living beneath the snake line, and our hopes have been that God will deliver us from the snakes. He does not do this by causing the snakes to go away, but instead by calling us to come up and to live above the snake line. In his book *"How to Stop the Pain,"* James B Richards puts it this way: *"We can pray as much as we like, but the suffering will not go away. We will not be healed of our pain. You see, God does not come to our vain imaginations to rescue us. He invites us to come to His reality, the kingdom of God."* God is not solely about delivering us from the snakes of depression, the snakes of sin, the snakes of poverty below the line in which they dwell. He is all about calling us to live from and think from a place where there are no snakes. He's calling us to live and think from His Kingdom.

Kingdom Vision

To be "Heavenly minded" is to have Kingdom vision. It is to have the King's vision and to see all things as He does. With having the mind of Christ, we are also being invited into having a vision that transcends the visions of this world. By God's Spirit, we are now granted access to seeing this world through the lenses of God. We can see what God has up His sleeve as it pertains to the future. To see as He sees, we must first acknowledge that our vision apart from Him has been way too low. We must then accept His call and an invitation to come up to a higher place in Him so that we may have Kingdom vision for His will here on earth.

> *"They serve in a system of worship that is only a copy, a shadow of the real one in heaven. For when Moses was getting ready to build the Tabernacle, God gave him this warning: "Be sure that you make everything according to the pattern I have shown you here on the mountain" (Hebrews 8:5, NLT).*

To truly grasp the significance of having Kingdom vision, we must not overlook what just took place with Moses. The writer of the book of Hebrews is using the story of Moses' encounter with God on Mount Sinai to reveal something amazing to us. This revelation is how the man-made tabernacles that were here on earth were just a copy of the real tabernacle that was in Heaven.

So here's the deal. While God was leading the Israelites throughout the wilderness, He then decided that He wanted to have a place in which He could dwell amongst His people. So what does God do? He summons Moses away from the people and calls him to come up to the top so that he may receive the instructions on building this tabernacle. In other words, these instructions could not be given and received while among the people at the bottom of the mountain. They could have only been received once he had come up to a higher place. It was there that Moses was able to get the instructions on what to build and how to build it.

Also, he was able to see into Heaven what had never been seen before. Moses was commissioned by God to build on earth what he had just seen. This commission is the call and the prerequisite to having Kingdom vision. We must first be called away from the mediocrity of our society and come up to a higher place in the Lord. Instead of going up to a mountain in order to co-labor with God, we are to now embrace a higher way of thinking. A low mentality will always produce a low vision. A high mentality will always produce Kingdom vision. We arrive at this Kingdom vision by allowing His Spirit to lead us into the visions of God.

"The voice said, "Come up here, and I will show you what must happen after this." And instantly I was in the Spirit, and I saw a throne in heaven and someone sitting on it" (Revelation 4:1-2, NLT).

The Apostle John was also summoned by God to first "come up" so that he would be able to see what God's next move was. Then immediately he was led by God's Spirit and only then was he able to see into Heaven. It is the Spirit of God who guides us into having Kingdom vision and what is to come. *"When the Spirit of truth comes, he will guide you into all truth. He will not speak on his own but will tell you what he has heard. He will tell you about the future" (John 16:13, NLT).*

God is inviting all of His people to "come up" so that we may possess His Kingdom vision. Imagine with me for a minute that there are inventions and creations that are in Heaven that has never been seen before. God is waiting for someone who is willing to take the limits off of Him, and someone who would be willing to think outside of the box. I am persuaded that our job as believers with Kingdom vision is to build here on earth what the Holy Spirit has allowed us to see and hear from Heaven. It is having Kingdom vision that leads us to live distinguished lives.

Dreaming With God

All of us have had dreams in life, aspirations, goals, and ambitions. One of the clichés of the world has been to "follow your dreams." Someone's dream may be to own their own business, to write books, start a church, find the cure for AIDS, end world hunger, preach the Gospel or even become the president of the United States. Some of us may be in the middle of fulfilling our dreams; while some may have laid down their dreams for a moment. Regardless of where you are in your dreaming process, all of us have imagined and aspired to do great things that would change the world.

Dreaming with God is being willing to step out of the boat and leave the comforts of mediocrity while in the pursuit of greatness. To dream with God, we must allow God to use our imaginations to think outside of the box so that we may build God's kingdom. We must come to realize that God has dreams of His own for us all. His dreams and plans for our lives are to *"prosper us, and not to harm us but to give us a hope and a future" (Jeremiah 29:11)*. Ultimately, to dream with God is to yield to God's plans and purposes for our lives. Let's go back to our dreamer Joseph, for in his story is a great revelation that will help us all learn how to dream with God.

"Now Joseph had a dream, and he told it to his brothers; and they hated him even more." (Genesis 37:5, NKJV). In our English translations, this passage reads *"Joseph had a dream"* and this is how we have normally heard it taught. In the original Hebrew text, the passages are read backwards. This passage in the original Hebrew text can be read as *"the dream had Joseph."* Wow, let's think about that! The dream had Joseph! Lou Engle explains this as, *"Joseph had a dream, but really the dream had him."* We all have had dreams of something great before, but it is something totally different when the dream has you. For a dream to have you would be for your life to be overtaken by something that is bigger than you.

God has dreams and plans for your life. For God's dream to have you is for your life to be consumed with His purposes. I would like to imagine that Joseph may have had a dream, but ultimately it was God's dream that had him. What all would transpire with Joseph's life was just the fulfillment of God's plans. Dreaming with God is not just about God fulfilling your dreams. To fulfill our purpose in life is to realize that it's all about us fulfilling God's dream. It's all about His people learning how we are to fit into God's ultimate plan for redemption. When we yield to God and His plans, we will quickly realize that it was never us who had the dream, but it was the dream that had us.

When you have been overtaken and consumed with God's dreams for your life, His dreams will always outlive you. You will never live long enough to see all that He has promised come to pass within your lifetime. In fact, it will probably be the next generations that will serve as the benefactors of you dreaming with God. For example, Joseph lived long enough to see his God-given strategy for Egypt be implemented and for him and his family to be reunited. He knew that there would be a lineage that he served as an ancestor to that would one day leave Egypt and make it to the land that God had promised His people.

> *"Soon I will die," Joseph told his brothers, "but God will surely come to help you and lead you out of this land of Egypt. He will bring you back to the land he solemnly promised to give to Abraham, to Isaac, and to Jacob." Then Joseph made the sons of Israel swear an oath, and he said, "When God comes to help you and lead you back, you must take my bones with you." (Genesis 50:24-25, NLT).*

Let's look at Joseph's bones as the continuation of God's dreams that started with Joseph, but would end with His people the Israelites. By taking his bones, they were, in essence, carrying his dream with them until they reached the fulfillment of God's promises for their lives. This image should encourage us as well. Regardless of what God has promised you and no matter the various detours of life, continue to carry your dreams close to you until you see all that God has promised come to pass in your life. Remember, *"He who promises is faithful!"* Joseph's dream outlived him, and it was one day that the Israelites was able to enter the Promised land with Joseph's bones (Joshua 24:32) because someone dared to dream with God.

Let's look at the late and great Dr. Martin Luther King, Jr., who is famous for having a dream. We are the benefactors of Dr. Martin Luther King Jr.'s dream. Remember what I said; when consumed with God's dreams, plans, and purposes for your life, His dreams will always outlive you. The dream of equality may have begun with King, but we are now the benefactors of this dream. We are now still carrying this dream until we see the full fruition of it come to pass.

I would like to suggest that it wasn't Dr. King who had the dream, but rather it was God's dream that had him. That's why the late and great Dr. King could pass away, but the dream still remains alive today. That is because the dream didn't begin with him. It began with God, and he served as the willing vessel in which God's plans for humanity were given the necessary platform. I was once encouraged by a great leader within my life, Dr. Gideon Olaleye, to *"do something today that you won't live long enough to see."* This can only happen when we learn to dream with God and yield to His plans for our lives.

Big Ambitions

For the one who has learned to have the mind of Christ, they have learned to think big, dream big and never to settle for less in life. The more that we come to know about God and His plans for our lives, then more our expectations of Him should begin to grow. The bigger our ambitions in life should be. Many of us have heard the old cliché that "the enemy to greatness is good." The challenge for people who aspire to be great and progressive is that there are too many temptations along the way that can easily lure us to settle for mediocrity.

This temptation to settle was best illustrated with the Israelites as they were on their way to the Promised Land. There were two and a half tribes that had come to some land. They talked amongst themselves about not continuing to wait for the land of promise, but to settle instead for what was there. Let's check it out.

> *"The territory of Ataroth, Dibon, Jazer, Nimrah, Heshbon, Elealeh, Sebam, Nebo, and Beon, which the Lord struck down before the community of Israel, is good land for livestock, and your servants own livestock." They said, "If we have found favor in your sight, let this land be given to your servants as a possession. Don't make us cross the Jordan" (Numbers 32:3-5, HCSB).*

These tribes essentially decided that this land they had stumbled across was good enough for them. Their cry became, *"Don't make us cross the Jordan."* The east side of the Jordan where they wanted to settle was "good land," but the west side of the Jordan where the others were to settle was the "Promised land." They were all too willing to bypass what was promised for what was good. Keep in mind that in this "good land" they would have to build their own homes, cisterns and plant their own gardens. In the "Promised Land" the homes, cisterns and wells were already built, and the gardens were already planted. They did not have to work for their blessings like those who had decided to settle.

When we find ourselves settling for less than what God has promised, we will also find ourselves having to work and toil for His blessings. We will have to do more for less while we try to figure out why others were able to walk right into the fullness of His promises. It pays to never settle nor compromise on what we now have available in God. The mind of Christ doesn't settle for what is good. It dreams big, has big ambitions, and it waits on the promises of God.

The Wisdom and Creativity of God

Before we can conclude this chapter, we must explore the truths of the wisdom and creativity that comes with the mind of Christ. To have divine wisdom, creativity and understanding is to have the mind of Christ. It is to think like God, not according to the wisdom of this world, but according to the wisdom of God. There is a difference.

> *"Yet when I am among mature believers, I do speak with words of wisdom, but not the kind of wisdom that belongs to this world or to the rulers of this world, who are soon forgotten. No, the wisdom we speak of is the mystery of God" (1 Corinthians 2:6-7, NLT).*

God's wisdom is knowing the truths of God and life and knowing how to apply these truths. With having the mind of Christ, we now have access to see things, situations, and circumstances as God does. We learn to interpret our realities through different lenses. With His wisdom, we see our circumstances as they are. It is His Spirit who will guide us in knowing how to approach all of life's circumstances.

> *"And in all matters of wisdom and understanding about which the king examined them, he found them ten times better than all the magicians and astrologers who were in all his realm" (Daniel 1:20, NKJV). "Daniel distinguished himself above the administrators and satraps because he had an extraordinary spirit, so the king planned to set him over the whole realm" (Daniel 6:3, HCSB).*

In comparison to the wisdom in Babylon, Daniel was *"ten times better."* Where did this wisdom come from? The Bible says that He had an "extraordinary *spirit.*" It was God's hand on him and God's Spirit with him that caused Daniel to be distinguished from others. Let's look at how the rulers of this world responded to Solomon and God's wisdom in his life.

116

"She exclaimed to the king, "Everything I heard in my country about your achievements and wisdom is true! I didn't believe what was said until I arrived here and saw it with my own eyes. In fact, I had not heard the half of it! Your wisdom and prosperity are far beyond what I was told" (1 Kings 10:6-7, NLT).

It was King Solomon who was deemed as the "wisest man on earth." It was also said that the Queen of Sheba traveled months to test the wisdom of Solomon. He was able to answer every question of hers effortlessly. His wisdom drew the presence of kings and queens from all over the world to Jerusalem just to sit at his feet.

In the Old Testament they had wisdom that came from God, but now being under a greater covenant, we can be filled with the One who is wisdom, Jesus Himself. To have the mind of Christ is to be filled with Jesus, who is the wisdom of God. *"God has united you with Christ Jesus. For our benefit God made him to be wisdom itself" (1 Corinthians 1:30, NLT).*

Jesus Himself is our wisdom and with His Spirit, we are now able to have wisdom that Solomon, Daniel, and Joseph could have never imagined. We have God's wisdom so that we may navigate throughout the circumstances of life. We are granted this wisdom from God so that we may join Jesus in His work. Having God's wisdom is not designed to make you better than others, but it will equip you to serve them better and introduce others to God and His Kingdom.

With the mind of Christ comes the creativity of God as well. There's a level of creativity that every believer should exemplify as we are led by the Holy Spirit. Think about it. God is the One who created the world in seven days, and we are the ones who have been made in His image. We are supposed to reflect the creativity of the One who created us. The problem is that we have become too conformed to the standards of this world. We have allowed our surroundings to determine what all God can do through us.

Kingdom entrepreneurship and divine inventions should be at an all-time high. Inside of all of us is something that God wants to create and bring to fruition in this world. In the Old Testament days, it wasn't abnormal for the kings of other nations to come to God's prophets for strategies for war. What if this was the case now? Imagine the political leaders and presidents of our times coming to God's people for answers and solutions. We have limited the creativity of God that He has given to us by limiting His wisdom in our lives. Having the mind of Christ brings us to a place where we can see all of the potential and opportunities that lie all around us.

We end this chapter just as we started, with the Holy Spirit. It will be God who will begin to renew our minds according to His word and ways. It is through His Spirit of truth that we will begin to experience the shattering of strongholds and bondages in our lives. It is as we embrace the mind of Christ that we will begin to think victorious and live victorious. Let the *"mind that was in Jesus, be also in you" (Phil 2:5)*. Let's learn to live distinguished by having the mind of Christ.

6

Distinguished By His Heart

B y no means am I of any sort of a mechanic. Although I am aware of the significance that the engine plays to the mobility of a car. It is the engine that empowers the rest of the car. When the engine is defective, it will also affect the performance of the entire car. The significance of an engine to a car is the significance that our hearts play in our lives. In fact, I would go on to say that our hearts are the engines of our lives.

Perhaps there have been many people who have experienced what has been my testimony. Even after coming to Christ, it seemed as if my life was at times in a constant cycle of failure and destruction. No matter how many times I prayed, and others prayed with me; there were certain habits that were never broken. It seemed as if there was a quality of life that I could never seem to experience. There is definitely nothing distinguishing about a life that seems always to be put into park and never moving forward.

Just perhaps, I am not the only one who seems to have experienced this. If you can resonate with this testimony, then I have some good news for you. What people never told me was that the quality of life that I was continuing to experience was a direct reflection of what had been going on internally. What's happening in your life is an accurate portrayal of what is going on in your heart. In other words, if you desire to change your life, then you must first have a change of heart. It is important to know that you cannot change yourself; it is God who transforms you from the inside out.

> *"Keep your heart with all diligence. For out of it spring the issues of life" (Proverbs 4:23, NKJV). "Guard your heart above all else, for it determines the course of your life" (Proverbs 4:23, NLT).*

You have read it right. It is not our jobs, education, church membership, nor is it our finances that determine the courses of our lives. It is our hearts that determines the quality of life that we are to experience. Therefore, what we have been consistently experiencing in our lives, with our families, jobs, and relationships, are a direct reflection of the condition of our hearts.

You can give someone a financial breakthrough, but if they do not have a change of heart, it is inevitable that they will eventually go back to their original living conditions. If our minds are the steering wheels to our lives, then it is our hearts that are the engines to our lives. The consistent patterns and behaviors that you seemingly are unable to shake are because these things have become embedded within your heart. It is our hearts that determine the routes in life that we will take.

It is our hearts by which the issues of our lives flow out. What's on the inside will always be made manifest on the outside. Dealing with the issues of our hearts will probably be one of the most difficult things that we may have to endure. In order to live distinguished, it is necessary that we allow God to deal with, rule over, and work on our hearts.

Out of the Heart

> *"So Jesus said, "Are you also still without understanding? Do you not yet understand that whatever enters the mouth goes into the stomach and is eliminated? But those things which proceed out of the mouth come from the heart, and they defile a man. For out of the heart proceed evil thoughts, murders, adulteries, fornications, thefts, false witness, blasphemies. These are the things which defile a man" (Matthew 15:16-20, NKJV).*

What goes into a person is what will influence the heart, but what comes out from the heart is what defiles them. What comes out is an indication of what has been within us the whole time. The intentions of one's life, whether good or bad, is determined and brought to fruition by way of that person's heart. It's what's in them that not only comes out before others, but it will define who they are and defile them.

One of the essential jobs of our hearts is to project and manifest what has been occupying its space. The heart in itself doesn't discern what's good and what to allow in. Or what's bad for the heart and what to disallow. The heart's job is to process whatever has been allowed in and to bring it all into reality. Therefore, for us to live a distinguished life, we must be intentional in guarding our hearts. Whatever we allow to enter into our hearts will only be a matter of time before it will begin to influence our lives.

It is important that we are extremely watchful of what we are subjected to and allow to affect us. Even the subtlest things can have the biggest influence in our lives. For example, let's say that your heart has become persuaded in the Gospel of Jesus. Every day you watch and subject yourself to the morning and evening news. Whether you know it or not, there is likely to be an internal battle going on within you. Your heart has grasped onto the good news of Jesus, but every day you are tempted to succumb to the bad news that you are constantly seeing on the television.

You cannot assume that your heart knows which one to keep in and filter out. Once again, it is your heart's job to process and manifest whatever you have allowed to enter in. Before you know it, you are experiencing some good days and then the next day you are feeling low. Your life has become a spiritual see-saw.

This unbalanced life has been the case for so many people. I do believe it is because we have failed to guard what we have subjected ourselves to on a daily basis. When you allow your heart to be infiltrated with all of the bad news that is around you, then your heart will begin to make every effort to manifest this news within your life. If your heart is centered on God's good news, then God's goodness will eventually become your reality.

Every day, people are letting you know what's going on in their hearts. If you let people talk long enough, they will begin to express what has been consuming them on the inside. Subconsciously and without any effort on our parts, we are communicating the aches within our hearts. We are expressing the guilt and shame that we may be feeling internally. We are conveying the joys that we may have been experiencing. It is "out of the mouth that the heart speaks." Our mouths and our actions are just the microphones to the cries of our hearts. Our lives are just a projection of what has been going on inside.

Think about one of those old film projectors that we used to watch in school. The teacher would put the film in the projector. The images of what was in the projector would be displayed on the screen. The screen itself was not the film or the images, but it displayed the images that were within the projector. Whether good or bad, clear or distorted, the projector's job was solely to display what was on the inside of it.

This image of the projector is an accurate portrayal of our lives and our hearts. Your life is on public display before others every day. It is your life that is simply displaying the images of what is going on within you. So if you don't like what people have seen in your life, then now is the time for you to allow God to change the film, and project His plans for your life.

The Glass Ceiling of the Heart

Have you ever felt like your life was under a glass ceiling? No matter how hard you push forward and upward in life, you came to no avail. Perhaps you started to believe that there was some system or society that has decided to keep you down. To get ahead in life, you would need to "fight the system." Good luck with that! It's not a system around you that needs to be addressed. It's our hearts that needs to be addressed.

Out of our hearts *"spring the issues of life."* What's intriguing about this portion of the passage is that this word "issues" doesn't just mean the problems and difficulties of life. The Hebrew word for "issues" in this text is "totsa'ah" and it means "the outgoing, source and boundaries of our lives." This word speaks to how it is our hearts that determines what we experience in our lives and the boundaries in our lives. It is our hearts that controls and defines the boundaries of how high and how far we go in life. In other words, what's in your heart is what will establish the glass ceilings in your life. These issues and boundaries will always prevent you from experiencing no more than what is on the inside.

There once was a time where my family stayed at a certain resort, and we had to use our room keys to use the elevators. Now the tricky part about the room key was that your key would only let you go up so many floors before you would need someone else's key to get to the other set of floors. Our key would only let us go up to the 17th floor within a resort that had over 30 floors. Someone else's key would have given us access to the floors that our key would not. I would like to compare our lives to this analogy. Our hearts would be the room keys. Our hearts will determine how high we will go in life.

So in essence, when you find yourself praying like Jabez did when he asked for the Lord to *"expand his territory" (1 Chronicles 4:10)* in reality, you are asking God to deal with the issues of your heart and to expand the boundaries that lie within. Just as a fence determines the boundaries of a yard and how far the inhabitants within that yard can go, so it is with the issues of our hearts. It is the issues of our hearts that establish the courses of our lives.

Defining the Heart

Let's define the heart for a moment. Biblically, when the heart has often been mentioned, it is in the context of someone's inner being. The essence of that person. Not the physical heart that pumps and circulates blood to the rest of the body. It is more of the psychological aspect of someone's being. For example, let's look at the first and greatest commandment. *"You shall love the Lord your God with all your heart, with all your soul, and with all your mind" (Matthew 22:37, NKJV).* The word used for "heart" is "kardia." This word carries the meaning of "the center of one's spiritual life," and "the essence of one's thoughts, passions, desires, and purposes."

This word that is used for the heart describes what we know to be defined as the soul of a person. In fact, I'd like to imagine that when Jesus told us to love God with "all of our hearts, souls, and our minds," all of these were referencing the same thing. That is the very essence and core of who we are and all that makes us as individuals. Our hearts are our souls and the passions, the drive, the thoughts and emotions that make us who we are. Therefore, when Solomon tells us to "guard our hearts," he is trying to tell us to guard and keep our thoughts, emotions and our very soul from everything that would separate us from God's love.

"Beloved, I pray that you may prosper in all things and be in health, just as your soul prospers." (3 John 1:2, NKJV). Prosperity and health begins inwardly, and then it is manifested outwardly. It is when our hearts and souls are prosperous that

everything else around us will become prosperous. If you desire to experience God's prosperity, in all areas of your life, it is imperative that you make sure that His prosperity begins first within your heart. It is having a prosperous heart that causes you to have a prosperous life. If you have a healthy and whole heart, then out of your heart will flow God's wholeness. If you desire to no longer live a limited life and break through the glass ceilings in life, we must first invite God into our lives and let Him reign from within.

Throne of God

Then the question becomes, "how does my heart and soul become prosperous and whole?" "How do I begin to see God's wholeness in my heart?" It is first by coming to the realization that your heart is where God has always desired to be. What do I mean by this? Yes, God reigns from Heaven. Yes, God once dwelled in the temples made by the hands of men. It has always been God's desire that He would dwell in His people and that our hearts would be the throne of God. Paul's prayer for the church in Ephesus was that *"Christ may dwell in your hearts through faith" (Ephesians 3:17, NKJV)*. Paul's prayer should be our prayer as well.

Here's the problem. Regardless of how long you have been saved, in the hearts of men God still has to fight for that first place within our lives. A.W. Tozer said it best in his book, *"In the Pursuit of God."*

> *"In the deep heart of the man was a shrine where none but God was worthy to come. Within him was God; without, a thousand gifts which God had showered upon him. Our woes began when God was forced out of His central shrine and "things" were allowed to enter. Within the human heart "things" have taken over. Men have now by nature no peace within their hearts, for God is crowned there no longer, but there in the moral dusk, stubborn and aggressive usurpers fight among themselves for first place on the throne."*

Our Lord and Savior put it this way: *"For where your treasure is, there your heart will be also" (Matthew 6:21, NKJV)*. Even for those who confess to be followers of Jesus, there is still a tug of war for the throne of our hearts between God and everything else. Jesus also said that *"These people honor me with their lips, but their hearts are far from me" (Matthew 15:8).* This is not designed to be a moment of condemnation. It is a moment to bring even the most devoted disciple of Jesus to a place where we would remain conscious of the throne of our hearts, and who is truly occupying it.

Imagine with me that God, the Creator of the universe would desire to rest in your heart more than to dwell in a temple and the Heavens in which He created. So what does that say about your heart? It says a lot. We must no longer overlook this throne of which He desires. Our hearts are the throne from which He wants to reign. Remember, that what's on the inside of your heart will always flow from you and manifest itself on the outside of you. God's abundance of life isn't something that you stumble across, and that happens to you. His abundance of life was always designed to happen from you!

Makes the Heart Sick

A whole and prosperous heart from which God reigns has not been the testimony for most of us. In fact, it has been the opposite. Depression and guilt have been reigning on our hearts. Damaging relationships have been a constant theme for many of us. Even if we do our best to hide and masquerade our hurt, it eventually finds a way to manifest itself, and we end up hurting others. When we have become accustomed to living with a wounded heart, we tend to accept this as the norm and project our hurting hearts onto others.

"Hope deferred makes the heart sick, but a dream fulfilled is a tree of life" (Proverbs 13:12, NLT). When living life without Jesus, it is inevitable that you will develop a sick, hurt and wounded heart. In fact, Jesus is the only answer and solution for the miseries of our hearts. Heart disease has been one of the major factors in the deaths of so many people here in America and around the world. Imagine spiritually having a heart disease, never knowing it and still having to manage through life with a sick heart.

When we have come to learn how to live with a sick heart, then all of the other parts of our lives will eventually become affected. We will lack vision for our lives. Our relationships will remain damaged. Any progress in life will continue to be stagnated. Even if you were to accumulate wealth, you would still never have enough to fill the internal void that only God can fill.

Now the word "sick" in the mentioned above passage in its original language means to become "weak, tired, and grieved." It also carries the connotation to become "diseased" and to "show signs of symptoms." Now these "signs of symptoms, diseases, and weaknesses" may begin inwardly, but if the issues of the heart are not addressed, they will eventually manifest themselves outwardly in our bodies.

There are many doctors who believe that the majority of our physical ailments and sicknesses are what they would call "psychosomatic." Meaning that our cells and our bodies are just responding to the psychological, emotional and mental trauma that have plagued our minds and hearts.

When traumatic events and disappointments go unaddressed, they can begin to settle within our hearts. Eventually, the internal anguish within our hearts begins to manifest themselves as symptoms externally. For someone who has experienced a very devastating blow in life, just at the thought or memory of that event can cause overwhelming pains and discomforts.

Physical ailments are not the only manifestations that come as a result of a sick heart. In many ways, a sick heart has influenced us into habits, behaviors and lifestyles that are destructive. What do I mean? Oftentimes, we may use drugs, alcohol, or relationships as a coping mechanism for the issues in our hearts.

It may be the sick heart that influences someone you know to use drugs and consume alcohol. Others may see them just as a drug addict, and overlook that they are just someone who has not been able to recover from a wounded heart. For a young lady who has a promiscuous lifestyle, we see her as someone who has decided to devalue herself by going from person to person. Instead, we fail to see the young girl who never was healed from the rejection and abandonment of the men in her life. Her actions and lifestyle have just become the manifestations of a sick heart.

It is the condition of our hearts that will determine the courses of our lives. God never desired for anyone to live in a state of confusion. Confusion doesn't come from God. In too many instances, we have learned to live in a confused state due to the condition of our hearts. In our society, we have come to embrace lifestyles, which are beneath God's plans for our lives. And with having a sick heart, these lifestyles and habits just become the external manifestations of our disoriented hearts.

Hardened Heart

It is one thing to try to manage through life with a sick heart. It is a whole other set of challenges as we attempt to manage through life with a hardened heart. With a sick heart, we may at least acknowledge our need to be healed. With the hardened heart, we spiritually just drive past the doctor's office and avoid any assistance that may be used to cure us. When we learn to live with our hearts so cold and callous, it will cause the rest of our lives to be off centered and out of balance.

Imagine with me for a moment driving a car that has been driven over numerous damaging potholes. Due to these potholes, you are now in need of an alignment. Your car no longer steers in a straight and centered path. It forces you to put more effort into trying to drive straight. You are now putting unnecessary wear and tear on your car just because it is unbalanced. It won't be long before you will either be at a car shop or stranded on the side of the road.

When the blows of life have hit even the best of us, it can knock the wind out of us. If we do not address the pains of this life, and the sicknesses of our hearts, we will eventually become like this car. Every aspect of our lives will become off centered and out of balance. We will experience unnecessary wear, tear, and casualties in life. The cost of fixing our hearts will be more than we can afford to pay. There are too many people that have become accustomed to living their lives out of balance. In many cases, this is because they have learned to live with a hardened heart.

A sick heart and a hardened heart isn't just a byproduct of other people letting us down. What has caused many hearts to become damaged has been our frustrations with God Himself. It is disappointment with God and how our lives have evolved. Whether we admit it or not, many of us have some major trust and un-forgiveness issues with God.

So imagine the condition of the hearts of the ones who know that God is the one that they are to call on, but He is also the one whom they feel has let them down. God is the one who has allowed them to go through some serious and tumultuous situations, and in many ways, their hearts are now afraid even to trust God. This situation has become all too real for many people.

If I have just described you, then I would like to take a brief moment to encourage you. God knows what you are thinking and how you are feeling. He knows that you may be disappointed with Him, with life, others or even yourself. He knows that you may feel like you cannot take the risk in trusting Him or others.

Therefore, you have decided to cut yourself off from ever trusting again. Despite how mad, angry, hurt or frustrated you may be, God still understands where you are. He still loves you. He's not mad or ashamed at where you are and how you are feeling. He knows your heart even when you are trying your best to cover it up and appear as if you have moved on in life.

He is not out to punish you or to bring judgment in your life. He sent His Son to take your punishment so that you may have His life. Yes, there may have been many unfathomable things that have happened to you. Be encouraged that God is still a loving Father. Nothing that has happened to you has disqualified you from God's plans and promises. Regardless of the condition of your heart, God is able and more than willing to heal you, restore you and bring you to a better place in Himself. My prayer is that you would allow your heart to become sensitive to all of the ways that He has been good to you and displayed His unfailing love.

It is having a hard heart that has kept so many of us from experiencing His love, grace, and His goodness. It is not that God has decided to be good to some more than others. His goodness has been like the sunlight outside. Available and accessible to shine on every living being. The degree of shade that we may have hidden under will determine how much of this sunlight that we will experience. It is the condition of our hearts that determines whether we let God's love in and how much of God's love that we will experience.

For some people, they couldn't count on one hand how many times they have experienced God's love and goodness. While for others, there wouldn't be enough time in the day for them to explain God's grace experienced in their lives. What's the difference? The condition of their hearts. When referencing the "stony hearts" of the Israelites, the Prophet Jeremiah says that they *"shall not see when good comes"* *(Jeremiah 17:6, NKJV)*.

God's goodness could be staring at us in the face every day. Many times we would never recognize it because our hardened hearts have caused us to remain blind to God. It is when our hearts have been healed that we will then become more receptive to His goodness through Jesus. The condition of our hearts makes all of the difference in the world.

Separated From God

> *"Live no longer as the Gentiles do, for they are hopelessly confused.*
> *Their minds are full of darkness; they wander far from the life God*
> *gives because they have closed their minds and hardened their hearts*
> *against him" (Ephesians 4:17-18, NLT).*

Paul admonishes God's people to "live no longer as the Gentiles do." Implying that although you may be a believer in Jesus, you can still live as an unbeliever. You can miss out on the abundance of life that has been made available to you. God will not force His blessings of abundance on you. Experiencing all of God's promises will not be determined by God. Through Jesus, God has done His part, and His promises for your life are now "yes and Amen."

So what is it that hinders many of us from God's plans for an abundant and distinguished life? Paul would say that we have *"closed our minds and hardened our hearts."* It is our closed minds and hardened hearts that has separated us from "the life that God gives." The Gentiles were "alienated" from the life of God, which means they were cut off from God's quality of life. It has been the conditions of our hearts that have separated us from all that God has promised through Jesus. When you are in Christ, absolutely nothing will separate you from His love. If our hearts are not settled in God and His love, then we can hinder ourselves from all that God has desired to do with our lives.

I know that someone must be thinking, "Well, if my heart is sick or hardened, what must take place for me to have a healed?" Medically speaking, when someone's heart is in an unrepairable condition, there is only one hope for them. That is to have a heart transplant. That's right! To experience all that God has for us and to fulfill the life of significance that awaits us, we must recognize that we are in desperate need of a heart transplant. We don't just need anyone else's heart; people of God we need God's heart! This is where our heart's cry becomes "Lord give us your heart!"

Heart Transplant

Yes, we are in need of a heart transplant, which is a new heart. Our lives and our hearts without Jesus has been in such ruins that we are no longer in a condition to be fixed. Our lives must be exchanged and replaced with His. A heart transplant is an accurate depiction of what happened when we came to Christ, was filled with His Spirit and as we became a new creation in the Lord.

> *"And I will give you a new heart, and I will put a new spirit in you. I will take out your stony, stubborn heart and give you a tender, responsive heart. And I will put my Spirit in you so that you will follow my decrees and be careful to obey my regulations" (Ezekiel 36:26-27, NLT).*

So what is the result of this much-needed transplant? God will cause these new hearts to become "tender" and "responsive" to Himself. The areas and ways where we were unresponsive to God, He now causes us to be responsive and sensitive to Him. So the good news here is that He isn't waiting for us to try to diagnose ourselves, or fix ourselves. Rather, God has decided to take the first step and initiate this heart transplant.

So guess who the surgeon is? The Holy Spirit is the needed surgeon for this operation as the passage says, *"And I will put my Spirit in you so that you will follow my decrees."* We are not receiving just anyone's heart; God has now placed His heart within us. Having His heart is what allows us to feel all that He feels. It allows us to hurt when He is hurt. Rejoice over all that He rejoices over. This is where we will share in the passions and desires that our God has for others.

God's desires will become our desires as we learn to have His heart. There was once a story of an elderly gentleman who was in desperate need of a heart transplant. Fortunately for him, a compatible heart became available, and the heart transplant was a success. After learning to live with this new heart, he began to desire and crave some unusual things. This elderly man who was believed to have once loved classical music and fine dining was now beginning to long for rock and roll music, driving motorcycles and eating fast food.

What happened was that this man would begin to take on the desires of this new heart that had once belonged to a younger gentleman. The desires, longings and cravings that were in the heart of the younger fellow had now found its home in the life of this elderly man. This change of desires is how it should be for all of us who have had a heart transplant with God. His desires should become our desires. His passions our passions and the cry of our hearts should mimic the cry in Jesus' heart.

The Apostle Paul would call this the "circumcision of the heart." No longer are we to identify ourselves as God's people with an external circumcision with our flesh. Under the new covenant, we now identify ourselves as God's people with a circumcision of our hearts. It's having a new heart that will bring healing to the circumstances of our lives. With a change of heart, we will learn to experience a distinguished life from the inside out.

Now just because we are recipients of a heart transplant doesn't mean that we can go on living life as we once did. In doing so, we may cause ourselves to fall back into the same conditions of the old heart that we once had. It's one thing to have a change of heart. It's another thing to have a change of a lifestyle.

After someone has experienced a heart transplant, they would then be instructed to follow a certain regimen to continue the great health with their new hearts. As believers, we have some much-recommended regimens and disciplines that God has prescribed for us. One is to make sure that we have a daily intake of His Word and that we are consistently receiving His love. Let's begin to see His word as our daily medication.

Daily Dose of His Word

It is very important that we find ourselves becoming acclimated to the word of God. Learning to live a distinguished life is to know that it's not just about getting in the word of God, as much as it is about getting God's word within you. For a moment let's go through Jesus' famous parable of the "seed and the sower" (Mark 4:1-20). The parable is about God's word being sown into the hearts of people. It is about the abundance that comes as a result of having a receptive heart to His word.

It's the fourth soil in this parable that was referred to as "good soil." This soil is the condition of the heart that is fertile and receptive to God's word. It is with this soil that Jesus tells His disciples that His word will produce a harvest of blessings, *"thirty, sixty, or even a hundred times as much as had been planted" (Mark 4:20, NLT)!* Now this is the condition of the heart that we all desire to have. If you have been like me, you too have prayed that God would cause your heart to become this fourth soil. I mean, who wouldn't want a harvest of blessings of this magnitude?

"And He said to them, Be careful what you are hearing. The measure [of thought and study] you give [to the truth you hear] will be the measure [of virtue and knowledge] that comes back to you—and more [besides] will be given to you who hear" (Mark 4:24, AMP).

Here lies the secret to this "good soil." It is to the degree that you hear God's word, meditate on it, give thought to it and learn to apply it that will determine the measure of your harvest of blessings. It was never designed to be studied by one person and communicated to the masses only. It was designed to be read, studied, talked about, and meditated on daily. It was designed to be the dominating thought, influence and idea on your mind throughout each day. We are to do this for the purpose of being transformed and changed by God's word.

Fully Persuaded Heart

When God's word becomes settled within our hearts, we will no longer find ourselves being tossed to and fro by every doctrine, event, and circumstance. My testimony has been that one day I am trusting God, and I have peace. Then the very next day I am no longer trusting Him, and I am struggling with much fear. Perhaps, I am not the only one who has been on this spiritual roller coaster.

Why is it that I seem to struggle in my faith now as much as I did before I came to Christ? The answer to this question has changed my life forever and has revolutionized my walk with God. The key that positions you to no longer struggle in your faith and to live an emotionally balanced life is to have a fully persuaded heart. Faith is the belief in your heart.

Many people have defined faith as being our belief in God to do a certain thing. Our belief that He will fulfill a certain promise. Often, our faith is nothing more than hoping that God will come through for us. As great as these definitions of faith may be, they are not the totality of what faith is.

True faith has to be grounded in you wholeheartedly believing in what God has already done. What His Son Jesus has already accomplished through the Cross. To have a fully persuaded heart is to let the finished works of Jesus hold more weight in your life than any other force, thought or influence. When you are persuaded in what He has done, you will be less likely to doubt God in what He can do. We cannot afford to have a cross-less faith. One that is not centered on the works of Jesus.

Where there is a heart that is rooted in His finished works, there will also be a heart that is fully persuaded in His word! It is the illumination of His Word that brings us to a place where His works become a reality in our lives. It is the working of His word in our hearts that brings us to a place where we are fully persuaded. *"So then faith comes by hearing, and hearing by the word of God" (Romans 10:17, NKJV).*

A.W. Tozer says, *"And he would understand that while Israel looked with their external eyes, believing is done with the heart. I think he would conclude that faith is the gaze of a soul upon a saving God."* Did we catch this? Tozer would define faith as someone's heart and soul gazing upon God.

Faith in the Lord is when the beliefs of our hearts are fixed, focused and intensely gazed upon God, His Word, and His promises. When table scraps appear to be close to falling off of our kitchen table, our dog Princess' eyes are focused and permanently gazing at that piece of food. The house could be on fire, but no flames would be able to deter her attention away from this potential meal. It is the intensity of her focus that I would like for us to gain some insight on faith.

When we have become persuaded in the works of Jesus, the faith of our hearts is not focused on our finances, our jobs or even our health conditions. The faith of our hearts is focused and gazed upon God only. It is having our hearts focused on God that changes our circumstances. Our lives will be a reflection of all that God has promised. When trying times come our way it will be God's word within our hearts that will cause us to be *"steadfast, immovable, always abounding in the work of the Lord" (1 Corinthians 15:58, NKJV).*

Daily Dose of God's Love

> *"Jesus said to him, "You shall love the Lord your God with all your heart, with all your soul, and with all your mind. This is the first and great commandment. And the second is like it: 'You shall love your neighbor as yourself'" (Matthew 22:37-39, NKJV).*

Now that we have a new heart, along with a consistent daily intake of God's word, we are strongly advised to have a daily intake of God's love. As much as we aspire to love God and others as we are supposed to, if we are honest, this has been very difficult to do. It is one thing to have to love God first above all else. Then to follow that commandment up with the requirements of loving others as we would ourselves. Now that's a tall order.

What we must come to realize is that this isn't just the requirement of love, it is the results of love. Or in other words, we are to love God, others and ourselves as we have first received love. Therefore, if we are going to live life with a new heart, we must first have a heart that is receptive to the very love of God. Many people have never been taught how to simply receive. We have only been taught how we must give.

You cannot give something that you have not first received yourself. The Apostle John said it like this: *"We love Him because He first loved us"* (1 John 4:19, NKJV). It is one thing to know with our intellect and understanding about God's love. It is a whole other thing to have experienced His love and to have caught the revelation of God's heart towards us all.

"Now to Him who is able to do exceedingly abundantly above all that we ask or think, according to the power that works in us" (Ephesians 3:20, NKJV). For a moment let's begin to consider this promise as the epitome of what distinguished living looks like in the Lord. This passage is what happens as we are set apart for a significant lifestyle in the Lord. The passages before it serve as a set of instructions that is designed to help all of us experience God's "exceedingly and abundant" promises.

"That Christ may dwell in your hearts through faith" (Ephesians 3:17, NKJV). Be mindful that Paul did not say that Christ would dwell in our minds; instead, in our hearts. Too many people only know Jesus with their minds and with their intellect. To truly to know Him is to know Him with our hearts. It is only right that as Jesus dwells within our hearts, that we shall come to know of His love for us.

> *"May be able to comprehend with all the saints what is the width and length and depth and height to know the love of Christ which passes knowledge; that you may be filled with all the fullness of God"* (Ephesians 3:18-19, NKJV).

Notice that Paul says the "width, length, depth and height" of His love. This passage speaks to the various dimensions of God's love. In fact, His love has no ending point. Once you have thought that you have experienced all that His love has to offer, there is always much more! Where there is the revelation of His love, there is also an encounter with the fullness of God. Our distinguished living can only go as far as our revelation of God's love. Every day God is waiting for us to come to Him and remain open to His love.

Every day is another opportunity to experience His love in a new and amazing way. How is this done? *"Now hope does not disappoint because the love of God has been poured out in our hearts by the Holy Spirit who was given to us." (Romans 5:5, NKJV).* Our hearts become receptive to God's love as we begin to yield our hearts to His Spirit.

God never desired that learning to love Him back would require so much strain and effort. Giving love was always supposed to be the result of first receiving love. In order to receive love, our hearts must be open and receptive to God first. Our love for ourselves, our families and those who are around us should be natural and an extension of His love. Displaying that love to everyone around you is learning to live a distinguished life in the Lord. Having a distinguished life is to have a distinguished heart; one in which God's love can flow to, and God's life can flow through.

7

Distinguished By His Grace

A couple of years ago my wife and I were in a season that many people had found themselves in as well. We were in a financial crunch and strapped for cash. We were both employed, but with my employment, at the time the Lord would only allow me to work 20 hours a week. How could a man ever provide for his family with 20 hours of a week's work were my thoughts? It wasn't because these were the only amount of hours that were available, or that I had some physical handicap that would prohibit any additional work.

The Lord navigated my steps to this job. Being in a financial dilemma, we did like any other reasonable people would do. I eventually began to look for other places to work, but God would shut down those opportunities. Still, He would reveal to us that it wasn't my time to depart from where He had placed me. Then I began to look for a second job, but God would not allow anyone to contact me back, not even for the most menial positions. I was bewildered with why God was allowing this to occur, especially since we were faithful tithers. What happened to the windows of heaven being opened and blessings being poured out on our behalf? Where was our overflow?

God was certainly intentional about closing doors, even to working extra hours, overtime, and every other option. Then one day while at work, I inquired of the

Lord as to why He wouldn't allow us to pursue other avenues for financial stability. He reminded me of a familiar story of Paul and the thorn (2 Cor. 12:1-10). The thoughts came to me as if God was asking me about my familiarity of this story.

He would ask me, *"How many times did Paul seek me (God) about the removing of his thorn?"* Inwardly, I would reply back, *"Three times."* Then God would ask me *"And what was my response to Paul?"* For the record, whenever you find God asking you questions, it is not because He doesn't know the answers. Rather, He may be causing you to re-examine your answers, and He may be setting you up for a life changing revelation! So my response to His last question was, *"Well God, of course, you told Paul no to his request for the thorn to be removed."* Then I heard Him bring clarity to my response by telling me, *"I never told Paul "no;" my response to Paul was "my grace is sufficient."*

At this time, I was baffled and unclear of how to process what point God was trying to make. God then reminded me of all of the times that my wife and I had attempted to solve our financial concerns by our own means. The Lord continued to speak to me by telling me that He had been closing the doors on all of our various options. For two years He had been trying to introduce us to His grace.

The closed doors were designed to reveal His grace pertaining to our finances. He wanted us to experience how it would be His grace that would provide for us despite our lack of finances. In fact, I'd like to imagine that whenever you see a significant difference between what's coming in and what's going out, this discrepancy is an opportunity to experience God's grace. It is the grace of God that makes up the deficiencies in our lives.

Every place where there's a deficiency in our lives there is also an opportunity to be introduced to God's grace. It was Apple who when referencing the various functions of their iPhone coined the phrase, *"there is an app for that."* When referencing all that we would ever need in life to live distinguished, I would like to encourage you that there is a grace for that. So that we may live a full life of purpose, at some point we must become acquainted with the grace of God.

It can no longer remain just a famous hymn that we grew up on in church. The very grace of God must become a reality and a lifestyle. In this chapter, we will go further into all that makes up God's grace. We will expound on the grace of God that is intended to distinguish us and how to experience His grace practically.

What Is This Grace

For many people, grace has been something like that Christmas gift you got from someone in your family. You appreciate that you got it. You'd imagine that it serves some purpose in life, but you don't have a practical use for it in your day to day activities. Therefore, like that Christmas gift, you just set it aside until someone helps you figure out what it is, and all that it does. Well even greater than any Christmas gift, this gift is truly the gift that keeps on giving. This gift is the one that determines whether we will live a mediocre life or an abundant life in God.

Therefore, let's take a moment to explore further what this amazing grace is. The simplest way to define God's grace is that it is purely God's goodness at work in our lives. The term that is used to define grace in the Greek is "charis." This word "charis" means God's grace at work within us, His favor to us, and His kindness towards us. His grace is also seen as God's gift, blessing, and goodness brought to man through Jesus Christ. That's it. It is the goodness of God, specifically, His grace at work in the lives of those who aren't qualified for this goodness.

What God's grace is designed to do is to point us and others back to the goodness of God. In fact, when God had confirmed to Moses that he *"had found grace in His sight..." (Exodus 33:17, NKJV)* God then tells Him that, *"I will make all My goodness pass before you" (Exodus 33:19, NKJV)*. God refers to His grace and His glory as "all of His goodness." So when we refer to the very grace of God we shall paint a picture in our minds that He has relinquished "all of His goodness" into our lives. No matter what our circumstances may be, God is willing to cause "all of His goodness" to invade our circumstances.

Let's further expound on what this amazing grace is. Grace is a person. Who would that person be you may ask? This person would be Jesus Himself. Jesus the Christ is the personification of God's grace and goodness in the world.

Think about this for a moment. Jesus is the good news of God, and it is grace that is the good news of Jesus. Grace is and was the work of Christ that purchased salvation and redemption for all of us. When people may begin to explain all of the promises and benefits of God, it is not uncommon for people to say, *"Wait. This is too good to be true."* Our response to them should always be, *"No, this is grace. The very essence and the good news of Jesus."*

Let's imagine that throughout the four Gospels; Jesus was the embodiment and manifestation of God's grace. When doing so, we will get a greater understanding of the power of God's grace. For example, let's take Jesus' first miracle. He and His mother were at a wedding (John 2:1-12).

The wine runs out. Jesus' mother looks to Him to solve this problem, and then Jesus begins to perform His first miracle. He has the servants fill the jars with water, and He then turns this water into wine. What we see is that Jesus is God's grace on wheels. Wherever we may have shortages and lack in our lives, we can expect God's grace to show up and provide all that we may stand in need of in life.

Think about the story of the woman with the "issue of blood" (Luke 8:43-48). It says that she *"suffered for twelve years with constant bleeding, and she could find no cure" (8:43, NLT)*. To make matters worse, with her condition, she wasn't qualified nor allowed to be amongst the people or Jesus. As she touched the hem of Jesus' garment, she then became whole.

There may be certain issues within your life. Maybe past mistakes, failures, or disorders that may disqualify you for a blessing. It is the grace of Jesus that qualifies you for blessings in the eyes of God. It will also be God's grace for healing through Jesus that will make you whole. In all that Jesus did within the Gospels, the manifestation of grace was designed to point people back to the goodness of God.

> *"For out of His fullness (abundance) we have all received [all had a share and we were all supplied with] one grace after another and spiritual blessing upon spiritual blessing and even favor upon favor and gift [heaped] upon gift. For the Law was given through Moses, but grace [the unearned, undeserved favor of God] and truth came through Jesus Christ" (John 1:16-17, AMP).*

In the fullness of Jesus, we have received the abundance of God's goodness disposed into every area of our lives. This promise reminds us of when God told Moses that He would let "all of His goodness" pass by him. No longer do we need to hide behind a rock to see "all of God's goodness." We are now able to see His grace and goodness through Christ.

This truth and promise put us into the mindset that in Jesus we have one blessing following after another blessing. Imagine the waves on a seashore. It is guaranteed that after one wave in a matter of seconds another wave will follow. Even at night when you are asleep, you can hear the continuous waves coming upon the shore. This truth of the waves is also true for the blessings, gifts, promises and grace of God that we have in Christ.

In the church that I grew up in, I used to hear the saints say that, "every time I turn around, He keeps on blessing me." This old adage is so true. You want to talk about living a distinguished life. There is no greater way to live than to experience the fullness of God's grace. Grace is not just something that Jesus gives, but furthermore, it is something that He is. When Jesus is at work in your life, so shall His grace also be.

"For the Law was given through Moses, but grace [the unearned, undeserved favor of God] and truth came through Jesus Christ" (John 1:17, AMP). If Jesus is the grace of God, then it was also God's grace displayed on Calvary's Cross. Therefore, grace did not come to do away with the law, but it did come to fulfill it. Grace came to fulfill what man could never do in his own strength. Grace came to bring us into the promises of God. Now we can better understand why this grace is so amazing!

Manifold Grace

This goodness is manifested in a variety of different ways. If we fail to know of the various manifestations of God's grace, we will run the risk of limiting His goodness in our lives. *"As each one has received a gift, minister it to one another, as good stewards of the manifold grace of God" (1 Peter 4:10, NKJV).* God's goodness can be seen, manifested and experienced in so many different ways. This "manifold grace" speaks to the fact that God's grace is multi-faceted, multi-purposed and diverse.

Twenty years ago the average cell phone only had one function, and that was to make and receive phone calls. Although that is still the primary function today, obviously they do so much more. What you are spending the big money on when purchasing these phones is the fact that it has so many different capabilities. So if you were only to use these phones to make and receive calls, you would be limiting all that they were designed to do. This has been the case with God's grace.

His grace here is recognized as the "manifold grace" of God. The Amplified version of the Bible describes grace as being *"God's many-sided grace."* It is multi-faceted, multi-dimensional, and it serves in a multitude of purposes within our lives. The grace of God is like a Rubik's Cube. It has multi-sides, with many different colors. You can only complete it by looking at every side of it, and by every different angle. Remember that whatever you may need in life from God; there is a grace for it. Let's look at some of the ways that His grace is to be manifested before us.

His Favor

His favor is what we experience when we may not qualify for a certain thing. In spite of our disqualifications, God overlooks them and provides what is needed for our breakthroughs. His favor is what blesses us with connections that we would have otherwise not had on our own. God knows that in order to fulfill His plans, we will need His favor.

He favors us not because we have earned His goodness, or qualified for His blessings. Instead, He favors us simply because Jesus restored us back to a favorable place in God. Because of Jesus, we are the target of God's favor, and we are now on God's good side. The good news about this is that we cannot lose His favor with works when we never gained His favor with our works. It is not what we do that qualifies us for God's favor, but rather it is what Jesus did for us. Hallelujah!

There will be times where we may lack what is needed to move forward into God's blessings and promises for our lives. Whether it be your lack of finances, credit, education, or experiences, this is where God's grace comes in. This is where God's goodness makes the difference. This is where you will begin to experience God's favor through the "manifold grace" of God.

Now the question becomes, "what does God's favor truly look like?" Let's take a look. *"To the praise of the glory of His grace, by which He made us accepted in the Beloved." (Ephesians 1:6, NKJV).* This word "accepted" means to be highly favored in the "Beloved." Who is this "Beloved" one? This "Beloved" one is no one other than Jesus Himself. How did we become so highly favored in the Lord before God? As Paul puts it, by the "glory of His grace."

This grace, who is Jesus, is what makes us highly favored before God. Favor looks like being in a relationship with God and knowing that it was Him who first desired this relationship with you. Favor is to be accepted before God. Favor does not begin with what you have. It is really more to be defined by who you are in Christ and your position in Him. *"For You, O Lord, will bless the righteous; With favor You will surround him as with a shield." (Psalms 5:12 NKJV).* God blesses the righteous, which are those who are in Christ. Then He surrounds His people with favor like a shield.

One of the reasons why so many of God's people miss out on God's favor is because we have failed to see ourselves as being favored. We are waiting to receive things and prayers to be answered before we can begin to see ourselves as blessed in the Lord. Often, our perception of being blessed is contingent on what we have from Him more than who we are in Him. Not truly appropriating our identity as being highly favored will always hinder us from walking in His favor.

Learning to live a distinguished life in God begins when we come to understand how blessed we are in Him. It is that *"as a man thinks in his heart, so is he" (Proverbs 23:7)*. I would like to also say that as a man thinks in his heart so shall he have. To walk in the favor and grace of God, we must first come to embrace that God favors us in Christ.

His Kindness

The kindness of God is another manifestation of God's "manifold grace." In my best attempts to try to explain His kindness, I will not scratch the surface of how merciful, gracious and kind God has been to us all. That goes for those who are followers and those who have not decided to follow Him. Let's try to explain this. We were all separated from God at one point and had no desire ever to be restored back to God. Every ounce of who we were was dead to God and totally opposed Him in every way.

Before we would be forever lost in darkness, God stepped in, and made the first move towards a relationship with us. God sent His only begotten Son to die for us while in the midst of our sins. *"God demonstrates His own love toward us, in that while we were still sinners, Christ died for us" (Romans 5:8, NKJV)*.

Although life hasn't always been kind towards us, God has. Resist from judging God's nature through your situations. Instead, learn to judge your situations through God's grace. We should never confuse the circumstances of life with the will of God for us. Despite our circumstances, His kindness is still being extended to us daily in amazing ways.

Think about this for a moment. Who would lay down His life for the very ones who put His life on the Cross? Who would love those who could never love Him back in the same manner? Who would purchase the salvation of those who could never repay Him back? Only God, and He chose to do this through His Son Jesus. The Cross of Jesus best displayed God's kindness toward us all! So what is the kindness of God? It is His mercy and grace being relentlessly extended to us despite our sins, mistakes, or wrong lifestyles. Not expecting anything back from us except that we would only believe in Jesus.

"That in the ages to come He might show the exceeding riches of His grace in His kindness toward us in Christ Jesus" (Ephesians 2:7, NKJV). It is the grace of God in which we see His kindness extended toward us in Christ. When we were running from Him, it was His grace and kindness that caught up with us. It was His grace that overtook us and brought us to a place where we were finally able to receive His love. In fact, our faith in Jesus is just our heart's response to His kindness in our lives.

"Don't you see how wonderfully kind, tolerant, and patient God is with you? Does this mean nothing to you? Can't you see that his kindness is intended to turn you from your sin?" (2:4 NLT). It is His *"kindness that draws us to repentance."* If you struggle with having a sincere commitment to God, allow Him to be kind to you. He knows how to cause His kindness to set your heart on fire. He knows how to lead you to a passionate relationship with Him. He knows how to use His blessings to get us where He desires us to be. He wants to be more gracious to us than we will give Him credit for. Where you or your loved ones may be struggling in walking with the Lord, expect His kindness and grace to draw you into that walk and relationship that He and you have both always desired.

Grace for Sin

> *"But where sin abounded, grace abounded much more, so that as sin*
> *reigned in death, even so grace might reign through righteousness"*
> *(Romans 5:20-21, NKJV).*

If you have been like me, this has been your testimony. I sin, then I try harder to overcome those habits of sin. Once it seems like I may have a handle over those habits and shortcomings, I fall right back into those sins. It's like sin still has its grip on my life. That is until I came to experience God's grace. Where sin may be rampant in your life, God will give you His grace to overcome those sins.

His grace is also His empowerment for righteous living. We see and read about all of God's high and holy commandments. It doesn't take us long to realize that keeping all of God's commandments and holy standards is not humanly possible. I do hope that you have come to that conclusion already! When God's grace is at work in your life, His goodness becomes the dominating force and influence upon your heart, your motives, and your actions. His grace is what empowers us to do what we could never do in our own strength.

> *"For the grace of God that brings salvation has appeared to all men, teaching us that, denying ungodliness and worldly lusts, we should live soberly, righteously, and godly in the present age" (Titus 2:11-12, NKJV).*

It is His goodness that empowers us to live in the righteous and holy manner. Holiness is the byproduct of His grace. When it comes to those old sinful thoughts, habits, and ways, they serve no match to the empowering grace and goodness of God. Don't allow old unconquered habits keep you from living a life of significance in the Lord. Let His grace propel you to live above sin and empower you to live righteously.

His Strength and Ability

Now think about this with me for a moment. God sent His Son to save you, and He did. Then the same power that raised Jesus from the grave God placed within you. He calls you to greatness by calling you to follow Jesus. He gives you a new heart and the mind of Christ. After all of this, we are still giving the world the best of our abilities and trying to change the world in our own strength. God is not inside of us so that the world can see what we can do.

We have been called and empowered by God to show the world what He can do through us. This degree of strength, ability and power is His grace. Another aspect of God's "manifold grace" is that it is His strength and ability at work in us. Don't believe me. Let's go back to the original passage that I had initially mentioned.

"And He said to me, "My grace is sufficient for you, for My strength is made perfect in weakness," (2 Corinthians 12:9, NKJV). According to what Jesus tells Paul, what is this grace? It is His "strength," specifically where Paul would be weak. So what does this mean for us? As it was with Paul, God's grace is to be our strength, ability and power in our lives to carry out His will.

Here's the deal. Whatever God has called you to do for Him in life, He has also given you His grace to do these endeavors with His strength. His ability and strength empower us for more than just the traditional form of ministry. Ministry is no longer just tied to a church. It is now outside of the four walls and into every arena of life. Therefore, the athlete who has dedicated his public platform for God's glory should expect God's grace to excel in all that he does.

Stephen Curry, for the 2015 NBA Champion Golden State Warriors, is a prime example of this. Being a young man who is on fire for God, it was only a few years ago that many questioned his ability on the court. It wasn't long until he began to show the world what perseverance, hard work, and a great jump shot should look like. I truly believe that God's hand is on his life. Stephen Curry showed the world what God's grace looks like as well, as he became the 2015 MVP and the first unanimous MVP in 2016 while winning leading his team to the 2015 NBA championship.

The fullness of God's grace can also be seen through the career of the rapper Lecrae. Once only labeled as a Gospel rapper, he is now becoming accepted amongst multiple genres of music as he has climbed the heights within both the Gospel and Hip Hop charts. Yes, Lecrae is the epitome of hard work, diligence and being a great rapper. I would also like to believe that he has been a recipient of God's grace, favor, and creativity. Most importantly, he has learned to yield his life, career and craft to the very grace of God.

I am a huge fan of Tim Tebow. Not just for his athleticism, but more for his uncompromising beliefs. Everyone knows that he is a devout follower of Christ. Many may not agree that he has what it takes to be successful in the league. No one can deny the impact that Tim Tebow has had in college football, in the NFL and with his teammates in the locker rooms. If you were to ask me, Tim Tebow is the perfect example of God's ability at work within someone's life and career.

The grace of God may not cause you to run faster, jump higher, or even win games. His grace will give you the impact, influence and favor of those who do jump higher, run faster and so on. Grace is God showing others what He can do if He had your job, had your career and when He leads your life. When others see you, they should see His grace. When seeing God's grace, others should also see what it would look like if Jesus were a professional NBA player, a doctor, a scientist, or whatever your occupation may be.

If you are a student in school, God has given you His wisdom to excel in every course. It is His grace that will guide you to learn, retain, and comprehend all that has been taught. The great news is that we do not have to be skilled, or experienced in a certain thing to experience His grace. His grace seems to work best in the areas where you are not qualified or capable. Now we see why His grace is so amazing. For God uses it to make us successful, productive, and progressive in whatever we shall put our hands to do for Him.

Let's go back to John 1:16 where the Apostle John tells us that, *"And of His (Jesus) fullness we have all received, and grace for grace."* I love how John Bevere speaks to this truth in his book called, *"Relentless."*

> *"Suppose I approach a struggling businessman by saying, "We have a new scientific means of being able to give you the fullness—the full ability—of Bill Gates." What do you think that the struggling businessman's response would be? He'd cry out, "I want it! Let's do it!" What would he do after receiving Bill Gates full ability? He'd start thinking of ways to design new products and make business investments that he'd never thought of before. Well, grace hasn't given us any of the fullness of Roger Federer, Frank Lloyd Wright, or Bill Gates. That would be a grace far too small. No, God's grace has given us the fullness of Jesus Christ Himself! (pg. 33)"*

Wow, did you get that? God's grace is designed to reveal the fullness of Jesus' wisdom, strength, and power while we are serving others. What a privilege and what a promise. As amazing as this grace is we have not always exhibited this goodness before others. Let's explore some of the reason why many are not experiencing this amazing grace of Jesus.

Embracing Our Weaknesses

> *"Therefore most gladly I will rather boast in my infirmities, that the power of Christ may rest upon me." "For when I am weak, then I am strong"* (2 Corinthians 12:9, 10, NKJV).

To truly demonstrate God's grace and strength, Paul had to welcome his weaknesses. In fact, it was only after he began to embrace his weaknesses that the "power of Christ would rest upon him." One reason why the majority of us have not come to experience this degree of grace is that we refuse to embrace our own weaknesses and deficiencies.

Many of us have been raised to believe that being weak means being deficient and that something is wrong with us. Being weak doesn't mean that we are less than others. It just means that we are in need of God. Consider this for a moment. If God's strength is best seen where we are weak, then we can never expect God to reverse these roles. There's no ounce of weakness in God. Therefore, by the process of elimination, we are the weak ones. In fact, I'd say that God's grace and strength may be waiting for us to finally acknowledge our weaknesses.

Have you ever asked God to give you strength, and the very next thing that took place was that you were weaker than before your prayer? This circumstance might just be God's way of answering your prayer. Because it is when you are weak, that you are strong in Him! Walking in God's grace and strength is all about welcoming our weaknesses. Whenever we come to the realization of our own feebleness, we then position ourselves to be invaded with God's grace. Our weaknesses will always be the bulls-eye for His strength and power.

Independence From God

Another reason that has served as a hindrance to many experiencing God's grace is that we have tendencies to put our trust in our own abilities. We tend to trust all that we can naturally see more than what we cannot see. To get good grades in school, we will have no problem in praying to God. Eventually, we will trust our comprehension levels more than we would trust God to give us the mind of Christ. When in a financial crunch, we will have no problem making financial declarations from the Bible. At the same time, we will still trust in our ability to work enough hours, put in overtime, and get loans more than we would trust God to supply all of our needs.

God will never force the fullness of His grace into your life. Not trusting Him will hinder the very grace that God has intended to manifest in your life. Any area of your life where you are trusting in something other than God is an area where God's grace cannot freely flow. When we fail to trust God for our finances, we will miss out on His grace for provision. When we fail to trust God with the raising up of our children, we will miss out on God's grace and wisdom for parenting. Yes, it is our independence and lack of trust in God that will hold up His goodness and grace.

"Cursed are those who put their trust in mere humans, who rely on human strength and turn their hearts away from the Lord. They are like stunted shrubs in the desert, with no hope for the future. They will live in the barren wilderness, in an uninhabited salty land. "But blessed are those who trust in the Lord and have made the Lord their hope and confidence. They are like trees planted along a riverbank, with roots that reach deep into the water. Such trees are not bothered by the heat or worried by long months of drought. Their leaves stay green, and they never stop producing fruit" (Jeremiah 17:5-8, NLT).

We see that for the ones who *"put their trust in mere humans, who rely on human strength,"* will hinder the blessings and goodness of God within their lives. *"Blessed are those who trust in the Lord."* They will be like trees whose roots of their faith will grow deep into the river of God's grace. No matter how hot our surroundings may get, *"we will not be bothered by the heat."* The promises end with that our *"leaves will stay green, and we will never stop producing fruit."* This passage is what a distinguished life will look like when we come to put our trust in the Lord.

"I do not frustrate the grace of God: for if righteousness come by the law, then Christ is dead in vain" (Galatians 2:21, KJV). James B Richards, in his book called *"Grace the Power to Change"* says, *"When I try to do things in my own strength, I nullify, reject, and neutralize the grace of God in my life. God does not take it away from me; through my unbelief. I choose to depend on my own strength instead of His"* (pg. 136).

Maybe you are in need of an open door for employment. Don't make the mistake that I have made so many times where I trusted in my resume more than His grace. Quickly come to realize that it is His grace that opens doors. You just may find all of the other open doors that have been waiting for you to depend on God and His grace.

Grace By Faith

So now the question becomes, "How do I get to that place in God where I can finally begin to experience His goodness?" We arrive at this place by faith. Faith is to have a fully persuaded heart about God's goodness. As we come to trust God and have faith in Him, will also begin to experience the practicality of His grace.

Our faith must serve as the prerequisite to experiencing the fullness of His grace. *"For by grace you have been saved through faith, and that not of yourselves; it is the gift of God" (Ephesians 2:8, NKJV).* It was by the grace of God that our salvation was purchased. It is by our faith in God's grace that we were able to receive this salvation.

Faith is the way that we come to receive and experience everything else that His grace can do in our lives. For example, you have some bills that your finances cannot cover. You believe in God and His favor to cover what your money cannot. As you believe God for His provision, His grace is what will come into your circumstances to cover your bills.

Notice I didn't say that money will come to you. Never limit God to money. He can answer the prayers of your finances in any way He chooses. We miss out on His grace because we limit how He may decide to provide. When we come to trust Him, we will also begin to experience His grace for provision.

Regardless of what you are believing God for, as you come to have faith in Him, you will begin to see the favor, and empowerment of God consume every area of your life. God will use your faith to position you for the fullness of His grace. It shall be His favor, strength and goodness that will always follow after our faith. A distinguished life is one that has been marked by the grace of God through faith.

Focusing On His Grace

The challenge in living a distinguished life will be to learn to focus solely on God's grace in every season of our lives. To focus on God's grace means to set the affections of your heart on the goodness of God. This degree of focus may appear to be easy to do when every day is a sunny day. When our days are not so sunny, it can become easy to begin to focus on our circumstances than it would be to focus on God's goodness.

Especially when it appears to be nothing good about what we are going through in our lives. Despite our circumstances, we can continue to focus on God. We can remain conscious of what He's doing in the midst of our circumstances, and in what ways shall His grace manifest. When our sights have been set on Him, we will learn to stay afloat, even in the midst of life's greatest challenges.

We all know the story of Peter walking on water with Jesus (Matthew 14:22-33). Now let's begin to see Jesus as the grace of God in this story. Therefore, where was the grace of God on this particular day? In the middle of a storm and on the water. For the record, God seems to display His grace and glory in the midst of the greatest storms of our lives. Learn to embrace your storms, for it may be a set up to experience His grace in greater ways.

When everyone else stayed in the boat based off of their fears, Peter steps out of the boat because of his faith. As Peter kept his eyes on Jesus, he was able to walk upon the water, defy all odds, and walk with God in the midst of a storm. When Peter's eyes began to wander away from Jesus, the grace of God, and focus on the storm that surrounded him, then he began to sink in the water. As our focus is set on God, we will experience His grace that will empower us to walk on top of the circumstances that would normally pull us down.

When you begin to focus on everything but God's goodness, you will become overwhelmed by your surroundings. Our hearts should be so centered on God's goodness that nothing will be able to deter us from His blessings. Nothing should distract us from His promises. Having this form of focus comes by way of living a life of faith empowered by God's grace.

When Grace Gets Onboard

I always like to look at the boats within the stories in the Bible as our lives. In the story Jesus getting into Simon's boat, we shall see what our lives will be like when grace gets onboard. *"Then He (Jesus) got into one of the boats, which was Simon's, and asked him to put out a little from the land" (Luke 5:3, NKJV).* Oftentimes, we have experienced what life is like when Jesus is not onboard or in this case when we have not yielded our lives to His grace. Let's check it out.

> *"But Simon answered and said to Him, "Master, we have toiled all night and caught nothing" (Luke 5:5, NKJV).*

While depending on his own efforts, Simon's conclusion for the night was, *"we have toiled all night and caught nothing."* Many believers' jobs, ministries, companies and efforts are like Peter's before Jesus came along. We toil, labor and work hoping to get results, and sometimes we see minimum.

Has this been your testimony before? Sadly, it has been mine for many seasons. Many people can relate to Simon and his frustrations. Too many times we have worked 40 plus hours a week and come home with nothing to show for it. Or some have spent a multitude of years in school but have not been able to benefit from their degrees.

Perhaps, it has been that we have applied for one job after another, just to keep seeing closed doors of employment. Often, these are the results of when we have not allowed grace to get onboard. There will never be enough hours to work a job to obtain the blessing or breakthrough that you are trusting God to bring to pass. Remember that it is His blessings that shall come by "grace through faith." Simon ends his frustration by complying with the instructions of Jesus, and he decides to let down his nets again.

Let's see what happens next. *"And when they had done this, they caught a great number of fish, and their net was breaking" (Luke 5:6, NKJV).* He gets the blessing of a lifetime as he learns to yield to the grace that is now on his boat. It is God's desire that as we depend on His grace, that we would get the results that Peter experienced.

In one day, Peter's fishing business got upgraded. What would have taken days or even weeks to accumulate, it only took minutes to accomplish. This day the world got a chance to see what God would look like if he were a fisherman. What blessings of God are waiting for you to stop trying in your own strength and begin to yield to His grace? Regardless of where you are in life, today God is inviting you to walk into effortless victories by allowing His grace to get onboard.

The story doesn't end there. *"So they signaled to their partners in the other boat to come and help them. And they came and filled both the boats, so that they began to sink" (Luke 5:7, NKJV).* The grace was on Simon's boat, but the blessing was bigger than his boat. Others were blessed because of the grace (Jesus) that was with Simon. God's goodness in your life is not just designed to bless you, but to also be a blessing to others, and draw them to God's goodness.

God's grace will bless you so that others may experience His favor that is in your life. He will use you as a walking advertisement of His goodness. Not only did God's grace exceed Peter's ability, but it also exceeded what He could contain. Whether they know it or not someone that is around you is waiting for you to let grace invade your life, take over and flow from your life into theirs. Let's not keep them waiting!

"When Simon Peter saw it, he fell down at Jesus' knees, saying, "Depart from me, for I am a sinful man, O Lord!" "And Jesus said to Simon, "Do not be afraid. From now on you will catch men." So when they had brought their boats to land, they forsook all and followed Him" (5:8,10-11, NKJV).

Under the Old Covenant, you had to repent first and then you would get the blessings. Under the New Covenant, God will bless you and use the blessings to bring you to repentance. Remember before that I mentioned that it is His *"kindness that draws us to repentance" (Rom 2:4).*

Here is a perfect example of this. Simon experiences this grace of God through Jesus. He receives a blessing that he did not work for, and naturally, he develops a repentant heart before the Lord. God knows how to use His kindness and goodness to bring us to a place of repentance and change in Him.

Finally, we see that Simon was willing to forsake all and follow Jesus. Before grace got onboard, he was only a fisherman, but after grace got onboard and blessed him, Simon then became a fisher of men. What does this mean for us? After experiencing the grace of God, Simon left his job so that he may pursue his purpose. One encounter with God's goodness can radically transform your life and bring you to a place of fulfilled purpose in God. In fact, it was at this point that Simon would begin to live a distinguished life for Jesus, but it began with an encounter with God's grace.

The Currency of The Kingdom

The reason why we are not seeing the fullness of God's blessings and prosperity invade our lives, our churches, our communities, jobs and endeavors is because we are neglecting to receive His grace. In every nation, kingdom and culture there is a currency in which these nations operate from. In America, our currency is the dollar. In Spain, their currency is the "Euro." In Mexico, it is the "Peso." What money is to this world is what grace is to the Kingdom.

Grace is the currency of the Kingdom of God. The Kingdom of God functions and operates off of the goodness of God. Therefore, if we desire to see all of the promises of God's Kingdom come to pass in our lives, we must first learn how to depend on His grace and live off of His currency. If we can seek and pursue the grace of God like we do the money of the world, we would see more of God's promises, and blessings. We have attempted to make our money, credit scores, reputations, fame, and fortunes do what only His grace was designed to do. What our money will not do for us His grace will!

If the Kingdom of God were a bank, then His promises would be our bank accounts. His grace would be our currency, and our faith would be our banking debit cards. For it is by our faith that we shall make withdrawals of His grace. The goodness of God is what will determine whether we experience the inferior blessings of this world or the superior promises of the Kingdom. Never make the mistake of thinking that God will bless us apart from His grace.

You may not be wealthy or be a millionaire, but the grace of God will give you the influence and favor as if you were. You may have a smaller ministry than others. You don't have to be a mega-church in order to do mega-ministry. You may not be highly educated, but His goodness will give you the wisdom that books could never teach you. His grace is what makes the difference! Let's live distinguished by learning to live in His grace. Let's change the world by experiencing and displaying His goodness. Let's show the world Jesus!

8

Distinguished By His Righteousness

Learning to live a distinguished life has as much to do with who we are in God as anything else. You will always live out your identity, and who you truly believe yourself to be. Therefore, at some point, settling the questions of your identity must take place before you can truly live a life of purpose. Before you can truly live distinguished and live a life that has been set apart for significance, you must first come to know who God has made you to be, the significance of who you already are, and the identity that has been established by God.

If asked who we are in Christ, many of us would say, *"the lender and not the borrower. I am the head and not the tail. Above and not beneath"* (Deuteronomy 28:12-13). This passage would be a great answer. Some would say that they are *"more than conquerors"* (Romans 8:37, NKJV). Once again, this would be another great answer. If asked about being the righteousness of God, many of God's people would draw blanks. This is because we haven't always been taught what being made righteous means. For God's people to truly live a distinguished life in the Lord, this truth and revelation will be pivotal. In fact, all of these awesome attributes of who we are in Christ are just the extension of being His righteousness. Let's go deeper into this truth.

"For He made Him who knew no sin to be sin for us, that we might become the righteousness of God in Him" (2 Corinthians 5:21, NKJV).

Living a life of purpose and significance is first grounded in the fact that Jesus died for us. In His death, He has now made us the *"righteousness of God in Him."* This word "righteousness" means to be in the state of acceptance before God. The significance of this is that this acceptance from God is how we should begin to identify ourselves.

We are to identify ourselves now by God's acceptance and our relationship with Him. No longer do we identify ourselves by our performances, activities, and recognition in life. Living a distinguished life is to be identified by a relationship instead of our achievements. We must come to realize that our achievements now derive from who we are; the righteousness of God. The great things that we will aspire to accomplish will only be an extension of our relationship with God. When you truly understand who God has created you to be, you will gain a greater sense of clarity of the greatness that He has placed within you.

Let's go further into what it means to be made righteous and the true importance of this in our lives. Before Jesus' death, no one was made righteous before God. *"There is none righteous, no, not one" (Romans 3:10, NKJV).* In comparison to the high, righteous, and holy standards of God, there was nothing within ourselves that could empower us to meet His standards. Therefore, this is where the need for a sinless, and perfect Savior would come in. Obviously, this Savior was and is Jesus. He died to bring us back into a relationship with God, make us acceptable before God and to restore us back to our original identities in God. One thing that we have used to determine our importance is who we are connected to in life. There is no one greater to be identified with than God Himself.

So here's the great news. To be the righteousness of God is to be in right-standing with God. To be in right-standing means that you are now the target of God's favor and affection. To be righteous means that He has decided to favor you in ways that those who have not come to Jesus will not experience. When pertaining to your endeavors, goals, and aspirations in life, you will now have God's favor being with you in all that you do (according to His plans).

"For You, O Lord, will bless the righteous; With favor You will sur-round him as with a shield" (Psalms 5:12, NKJV).

So who does God bless and surround with favor? He does these things to the righteous. So who would the righteous be? The righteous would be those who have placed their trust and faith in Jesus as the Son of God. If you have placed your faith and trust in Jesus, then you are now the righteousness of God in Christ. Your expectation in life should be that God will bless you and surround you with His favor as a shield.

In being made righteous, you must believe that God is forever pleased with you. Ultimately, His pleasure has nothing to do with your consistency to keep certain spiritual disciplines. It has everything to do with the reality that you have acknowledged and accepted that Jesus died to make you in right standing with God. This truth is your identity in life, ministry, and in all that you do. Living distinguished is learning to embrace who you are and that you are now made righteous in Christ.

Jesus' Righteousness

We are now able to rest in a true relationship with God based on what Jesus has done for us. Nothing can separate us from God's love and favor. Our position in Christ is a permanent one, and nothing can change that. Our position, identity, and favor is solely contingent and established in the finished works of Jesus.

So in essence, we are living off of Jesus' righteousness, and because we are in Him, and He is in us, the Father has no choice but to receive us as He has received Him. Our identities cannot be any different than Jesus' identity. *"Love has been perfected among us in this: that we may have boldness in the day of judgment; because as He is, so are we in this world" (1 John 4:17, NKJV).* As Jesus is right now, so are we in Him. Once again, this is all because of His works, and as an extension of His righteousness.

To describe or compare how we benefit from the righteousness of Jesus with God, imagine that the Kingdom of God was a bank, and we are now living off of Jesus' credit score with God. Stay with me for a moment. Yes, Jesus' credit score; Jesus has A-1 credit with the Father. *"And suddenly a voice came from heaven, saying, "This is My beloved Son, in whom I am well pleased" (Matthew 3:16, NKJV).* The fact that we can "go boldly before the throne of God" is because we are going to God off of Jesus' credit, works and relationship with the Father.

Let's say that if you ever wanted to meet me personally, or gain some form of favor with me, it would be wise to come to me through my wife. The one who knows me best and the one that I have a hard time saying no to. To go through my wife would be to get on my good side. The same is true with God. We are now on God's good side because we have come to Him through His Son Jesus. Truly there is no other way to get to God but through Jesus.

Have you ever received those "you are pre-qualified" notices in the mail? Those letters that have said that you are qualified with the bank for something that you have not even applied for. When you received these notices, these establishments have used some information or your track record to pre-approve you to do business with them. When being the extension of Jesus' righteousness, this is what life and a relationship with God is like.

In Christ, you are already pre-approved to do business with God for His Kingdom. You are already pre-qualified for God's promises and blessings. Through Jesus, you are already favored, blessed and made righteous with God. How amazing is that? This is the good news of Jesus and the extension of being Jesus' righteousness. Life looks much different now when we begin to identify ourselves as the righteousness of God through Jesus. We can no longer measure God's love for us by our circumstances. We must now know that He loves us by what Jesus has done for us. Living righteously is now the result of being righteous. Becoming righteous before God is now the result of our faith in His Son.

Righteous By Faith

> *"Yet we know that a person is made right with God by faith in Jesus Christ, not by obeying the law. And we have believed in Christ Jesus, so that we might be made right with God because of our faith in Christ, not because we have obeyed the law. For no one will ever be made right with God by obeying the law" (Galatians 2:16, NLT).*
> *"God treats everyone alike. He accepts people only because they have faith in Jesus Christ" (Romans 3:22, CEV).*

The New Testament is full of scriptures that seem to repeat themselves about how we obtain God's righteousness. I'm not sure how we can continue to read and preach from God's word and continue to overlook that we are made right with God by faith alone. I love how the Contemporary English Version puts *Romans 3:22,* *"He accepts people only because they have faith in Jesus Christ."* God accepts us "only because we have faith in Jesus."

That's pretty simple, right? To me, sermon messages on being righteous were mainly just a bunch of unexplained religious jargon. I use to hear statements and passages like these, and I would not have any problems agreeing with them. "Of course, it's my faith that makes me righteous," I would say. That is until the Lord began to show me all of the ways in which I was trusting in something else to make me acceptable to Him.

I used to think that I would have to pray certain prayers every morning for a specific amount of time in order to be pleasing to God. If I didn't pray these prayers ritualistically every day, then there would be some degree of blessings that I would miss out on each day. I thought that I had to read the Bible every day in order to remain blessed by God, and if I didn't, then God would be mad at me. I thought that if my attendance in the church was consistent, then I was fulfilling my religious obligations to God.

So here's the problem with these things and with this mindset. As great as these principles may be, if it is the demonstration of these behaviors that makes me right with God, then I have officially crossed over into a works mentality. I have now made my relationship with God legalistic, and my works and efforts are now the things that qualify me for God's blessings. Jesus' works are no longer enough for God to bless me. There must be some other things that I must do to be righteous. My righteousness in God is not by faith anymore. It is now by my works. Whenever I take on this mindset, I am also running the risk of canceling out God's grace and favor in my life as well. It is my faith in Jesus that qualifies me before God and causes me to be righteous in Jesus.

Someone may have a hard time receiving the fact that it isn't their church attendance, service in ministry, prayer time nor Bible reading that makes them righteous. Someone may be thinking that they would rather remain in works and try to fulfill their righteous obligations by doing these great things instead of just trusting that it's their faith that makes them righteous. They can't take the risk in believing that their faith is all that God initially wanted and not their works. They have a hard time believing that their works are an extension of their faith.

My encouragement to these believers would be that I once thought that way before as well. Until the Holy Spirit began to show me that it wasn't my obedience that made me right before God. It wasn't what I am doing that caused God to bless me. Instead, it is what Jesus had done that caused God to bless me.

"For as by one man's disobedience many were made sinners, so also by one Man's obedience many will be made righteous" (Romans 5:19, NKJV). It is not our obedience that makes us righteous, but it was Jesus' obedience on our behalf and our faith in His finished works. In fact, our righteousness is an extension of His obedience, and our obedience is the result of our righteousness. Therefore, I spend time in God's word, not to be righteous in God. Instead, I do this because I am righteous in God.

I don't go to church to fulfill an obligation to God. I do so because of my gratitude to Him for blessing me despite my attendance. I don't spend time in prayer to get blessings. Rather I do so because I am blessed. Your works for God is not what makes you righteous. It's the fact that you are already righteous in Christ that compels your heart to do all of these works. In the Old Testament, they had to keep the law to be acceptable, pleasing and righteous before God. Because of what Jesus did on the Cross and the grace that we are under, we now keep the law because He has already made us righteous. It shall be His grace that empowers us to live out God's holy and righteous standards before others.

One thing that I have heard all of my life was that for God to bless His people, we had to pay our tithes and offerings. It is a great practice to do. My mindset was that if I did this then God would be pleased with me, and I would be entitled to His blessings. As righteous as this act may be, I have come to realize that it can become works as well. Any acts of works and legalism that we exhibit can be the mentalities and acts that hinder God's blessings because we feel like we have to work to obtain His promises.

I have heard so many people who have dealt with financial issues say something like, *"God is supposed to bless me because I am a tither."* In other words, the fact that I am giving means that God owes me, and my giving is what entitles me to financial blessings. Not what Jesus has done, but the fact that I have fulfilled my religious obligations. Under the new covenant that has been established through Jesus, God now desires "cheerful givers" and not those who give out of obligation, or "necessity" as we have been trained to do. I believe that it has been our legalistic teaching of giving that is hindering many of God's people from walking into God's promises, blessings, and overflow. When you begin to live as the righteousness of God, being a "cheerful giver" becomes a condition of your heart and not just a religious obligation.

As we receive what Jesus has done for us by faith, our hearts will become cultivated in the ways of God. Any area of your life in which you are not persuaded that what Jesus has done for you on the Cross is not enough will be an area where you will revert back to legalism. You will then run the risk of "frustrating the grace of God" in your life. Just as we come to experience His grace by faith, we also will become God's righteousness by faith as well. It is the "just that shall live by faith" and not by their works.

Younger Brother And The Older Brother

Many of us are aware of Jesus' parable of the "Prodigal Son." Not necessarily focusing on the backslidden state of the younger brother, but let's fast forward through this story to the older brother's attitude. The younger brother "comes to himself" and returns home. The father sees this son as he is returning and he runs out to meet his son who had fallen by the wayside. Here is a great place to stop and encourage you or someone that you may know. Even if you have strayed away from God, He is always waiting for your return back to Him. Although we may have left Him, He has never left us and just as we see with the younger brother, God awaits our arrival with open arms.

As open as His arms were for the younger brother, the father wasn't empty handed either. He came with gifts! Once the older brother had asked one of the servants what was going on, he became furious that the brother who had left his father's house now comes back, and he gets all of the gifts and blessings. Let's look at his frustration as he confronts his father about this.

> *"But he said to his father, "For years I have worked for you like a slave and have always obeyed you. But you have never even given me a little goat, so that I could give a dinner for my friends. This other son of yours wasted your money on prostitutes. And now that*

he has come home, you ordered the best calf to be killed for a feast"
(Luke 15:29-30, NLT).

Let's be honest for a moment. Most of us would have probably responded in a like-minded manner.

So here's the older brother's problem. He had been faithful. Never once had he broken any of the father's commandments. He had never left the father's side. When the one who had left the father to live in a riotous manner came back, he gets the hook-up, and the father rolls out the red carpet for him. If anyone deserved this treatment, surely it was the older brother, right? Let's see how the father responded. His father replied, *"My son, you are always with me, and everything I have is yours"* *(Luke 15:31, NLT).*

The blessings of the father were there to be experienced the whole time. This older brother never had to work for what was always there. What we should take away from this is the one who had done nothing to deserve these blessings (younger brother) except come back to his father, was the one who had received this royal treatment. The one who had thought that all of his works should have earned him these blessings, (older brother) was the one who had to find out the hard way that the father's heart could not be worked for.

This story is a classic case of a works mentality versus grace and how when we use our works, and efforts to earn God's blessings we may experience the opposite. Just as it was with the younger brother who did nothing to deserve the blessings and only desired to be with his father, he was the one who received the goodness of His father.

This story has been recognized as the parable of the "Prodigal Son," but nowhere in the story did Jesus signify which one was the "Prodigal Son." I would like to suggest that just as the decisions of the younger brother had separated him from the goodness of his father, so was the legalistic works mentality of the older brother that could have kept him from experiencing this same goodness. We must no longer make the mistake that our right-standing with God is to be contingent on our faithfulness, works and efforts. It is simply based on our willingness to receive what Jesus has done on our behalf.

New Creation

Coming to the realization of what it means to be a new creation in Christ is also essential to living a distinguished life. For the longest, I knew what it meant to be saved in Christ, but I failed to realize what it meant to be a new creation in Him. Therefore, I could never move beyond the old habits, influences, and circumstances. Because I failed to realize that in Jesus I was made new, I reverted back to living in the old. If there is one thing that would hinder God's people from living a life of significance in the Lord, it would be the fact that we are missing out on the reality that in Him we have become a new creation. *"Therefore, if anyone is in Christ, he is a new creation; old things have passed away; behold, all things have become new" (2 Corinthians 5:17, NKJV).*

Oftentimes, we still deal with some old habits, or we experience more downs in life than ups. We may allow depression, fear, guilt, shame or low self-esteem to overwhelm us. Although the enemy definitely has a part to play in this, I would like to suggest that the majority of this up and down rollercoaster life is the result of having an identity crisis. In fact, I would like to believe that the problem is that we are waiting for God to deliver us from a battle that He has already won. We spend all of our lives trying to become something that God has already made us to be. We spend all of our lives becoming instead of just being.

We fail to realize that in Christ we have already become a new creation in Him and that old things have passed away, and everything has become new. We have this tendency to see ourselves as we appear in the mirror. We fail to believe what God's word has declared us to be. Or we tend to limit and define ourselves by our past, our mistakes and failures instead of identifying ourselves by His victory.

When Jesus went to the Cross, He went not just with our sins, but as our sins. He went as our old natures and died as our old natures. As we put our trust in Him and give Him our lives, in exchange we would receive His life and His new nature. One that is holy, pure, spotless and blameless before God. When we fail to realize that He died as our old sinful nature so that we would become His new holy nature, then we will always revert back to our old lives, old ways of thinking and our old ways of living. This truth is pivotal when learning to live a distinguished life.

Here's the good news! We do not have to carry with us the old baggage of our past. We do not have to allow our past to hinder our futures, nor do we have to live with our mistakes and failures. This is because, in Jesus, our "old things have passed away." This doesn't mean that we didn't do these things in our past. What it means is that when we died with Christ, we died to everything that we once did, and the impact that it had on our lives. These things no longer define who we are. Our old mindsets have passed away. Our old habits have passed away. Our old influences, sins, mistakes, friendships, and purposes have passed away. In Christ, "everything has become new!"

Now that we are the righteousness of Christ, our future, destiny and purpose in life are all new. In Jesus, we have a new mindset, a new mentality and a new way of living. I'm not sure how your family or friends may have been before you came to Christ, but now you have a new family better known as the body of Christ. You now have a new message for your family members and friends, and that is the message of redemption. You are no longer to be defined by the "old things that have passed away." Your identity is now grounded in the One, who has made you into a new creation.

For a moment, imagine with me the old life of a caterpillar and the new life of the butterfly. Think about all of the challenges that may be presented if the butterfly failed to realize that it was a new creation. The butterfly that was a caterpillar at one time was limited to living in low places and having to survive on the ground. It eventually goes through this transformation period better known as a metamorphosis. Once the caterpillar has become this beautiful butterfly, it must become acquainted with a new life and a higher way of living.

If this butterfly failed to realize that a transformation has taken place, then it may likely revert back to the old life, position itself to danger and live less than it was designed to live. This is the case for many of God's people after they have come to Christ. We have failed to recognize our own transformation in the Lord, and we have failed to live the victorious life we were designed to live. All because we have failed to realize that God has made us into a new creation in the Lord.

As A Man Thinks

"For as he thinks in his heart, so is he" (Proverbs 23:7, NKJV). Here's the bad news and the good news. However, you see yourself is how you will be, and this will determine the routes in life that you will take. If you see yourself as less than what God has created you to be, then this is what you will eventually become in life. If you are persuaded on who you are in Jesus, living the newly created life in Christ

is what you will live. The problem is that we are expecting new creation promises and blessings to flow out of an old creation's life and mindset.

You may have been able to masquerade yourself by the clothes that you wear, the crowd that you have surrounded yourself with, or even the accomplishments that you may have achieved. You may have been able to use these things to convince yourself of being one thing in your mind. If you see yourself as being different than all of these things in your heart, it will only be a matter of time before you will begin to live out this identity that you have attempted to cover up. In fact, we will never be able to escape how we see ourselves within our hearts. It is all about how you see and think of yourself from within that will determine the quality of life that you will live. I believe that God designed it this way; how you have identified yourself within your heart is how you will live before others.

Remember, that life was always designed to flow from you. *"Keep your heart with all diligence, for out of it spring the issues of life" (Proverbs 4:23, NKJV).* From our hearts "flow the issues of our lives," and so do our identities. Therefore, if you have become persuaded in your heart that you are now a new creation, then from your heart will flow this quality and identity of life. No longer will you need to use your accolades to define who you are or to build your self-confidence.

In all actuality, in having the revelation of your new God-given identity within your heart, the achievements in life will be a result of who you are. Even without all of the accomplishments, fame or fortune that life can offer, when you see yourself as God sees you, you can still have a great sense of self-confidence, unlike those who have to use their fortune and fame to feel significant. The more you come to acknowledge that you are a new creation in Christ, the more that you will also begin to experience the fullness of a new life in Jesus.

Favor Tied To Your Identity

Another thing that has hindered so many of God's people from experiencing God's favor is that we have failed to understand our true identity. When you come to realize the works that Jesus has finished on your behalf, then you will also realize that your identity is settled in God. You will also come to the realization that your season or circumstances never determine your blessings in God. Rather, your blessings in life will always be a result of the works of Jesus and your new righteous identity. Using a scripture that was mentioned before in *Psalms 5:12, NKJV, it says that God will "bless the righteous; With favor, You will surround him as with a shield."*

These blessings from God and His favor are given to the righteous. When we truly catch the revelation that we are forever made righteous before God, then we will also come to experience the favor, and blessings that are to belong to the righteous. Whenever I find someone who is struggling with God's favor, it is usually grounded in the fact that they are also struggling with receiving that they are the righteousness of God. Just know that God has tied His favor to your identity, and maybe His next great move of blessings are waiting for you to truly believe and receive who you are in God.

When His Righteousness Is Bigger Than You

It's one thing for God to use the works of His Son to bless you, make you righteous in Christ and acceptable before Himself. It's another thing for God to use the righteousness on your life to bless others, draw people closer to Himself, and bring glory to His name. This is exactly what God had in mind when making you His righteousness. He has always desired for His righteousness in your life to be bigger than you, and that the blessings that He has extended to you would also be extended to those who do not know Him.

Living distinguished is living a life where we are forever pleasing, acceptable and favored before God. Others experiencing God's goodness as an extension of our relationship with God is what takes living a distinguished life to another level. Imagine with me someone who has a membership to a certain store, shopping center, or fitness gym, and based off of his or her membership; someone else would be able to experience the perks of that person's benefits. If this would serve as an accurate example, then this is what it means when God's righteousness is bigger than you.

His righteousness will always exceed your own life because God desires to use your walk to get to someone else. Paul explains it this way, *"and that is as God was using Jesus to reconcile the word back to Himself, it is Jesus who uses us to call those who are lost to Himself"* (2 Corinthians 5:18-19, NLT). Paul calls our message to the world the "ministry of reconciliation." This message is not just to be preached or spoken to others, but rather lived out and demonstrated as we share God's love with the world. God's blessings in our lives were never designed to be a reservoir.

His blessings were always designed to be a river. In other words, His blessings and righteousness aren't just for you to experience, but it is so that others may experience them through you.

What Our Nation Really Needs

It is normal nowadays to hear God's people expressing their frustrations with this nation. I'd imagine that all of us have experienced this frustration. It goes without saying that things can be much better, and there is much work to do. Here is my problem with this. We are all waiting for our government leaders, and politicians to change in order for this nation to turn around.

Of course, there will be a need for our leaders to change and turn to God. What we seem to forget is that this change is first to begin with us. Ultimately, I believe that the much awaited and needed turn around in this nation will not come from those that we have elected and placed our trust in, but rather the change of this great nation will first begin with the church. This nation cannot fix itself, but that is why He left us in this world. That is, to point every society back to the only one who can truly change our circumstances.

> *"Then if my people who are called by my name will humble themselves and pray and seek my face and turn from their wicked ways, I will hear from heaven and will forgive their sins and restore their land." (2 Chronicles 7:14 NLT)*

Notice that it didn't say if the world will humble themselves. Instead, it said, "if my people will humble themselves." God has left us in charge of the affairs of this world. When we fail to realize who we are in Christ, we will always relinquish this call and responsibility to those that we have placed into an office. God's people have been charged by God to join Him in His work in turning this world's wrongs into rights and restoring God's lost children back to God.

"Righteousness exalts a nation, but sin is a reproach to any people" (Proverbs 14:34, NKJV). His righteousness in your life is what God will use to help raise the standards of our communities. God's righteousness within our lives is what He has decided to use to save those who are lost. *"If people are in trouble and you say, 'Help them,' God will save them" (Job 22:29, NLT)* When you have become

the righteousness of God in Christ Jesus, you will find yourself in predicaments where God is waiting for you to cry out on behalf of others so that He will move in their lives.

In no way does God need us in order to move in this world, but He has decided to use our righteousness in Him as an extension of His grace and mercy. What would it look like if all of us came to the realization of God's acceptance? Perhaps this nation would return to being "one nation unto God." Maybe the change in this country is waiting for us to wake up and realize the awesome identity that God has given us through His Son Jesus. If we were to realize that God has made us "accepted in the Beloved (Jesus)," we may just be the generation where the righteous standards of God will become the standards of this world.

Through the works of Jesus, God has finished and accomplished so much in this lifetime that we will never truly understand all that we have in Christ. I would like to challenge you to try to spend the rest of your days allowing God to show you who you are in Him. There is a life of greatness waiting for you to recognize that in Christ, you have been made righteous with God. The degree that you walk in your righteousness will determine the degree of favor that you will experience.

Living a life of significance is when we will begin to realize that it is not our performance or works that please God. Living distinguished is when we realize that it is what Jesus has done for us that makes us righteous. Living distinguished is when we come to acknowledge that as Jesus is, so are we in this lifetime. That is that we are forever righteous in God.

9
Distinguished By God's Kingdom

When it comes to the truths and concepts of the Kingdom of God, I was in the dark and knew nothing about this Kingdom. Of course, I saw it in the Bible and read about all of the parables in which Jesus referenced this Kingdom. Like many others, I was just thinking that our Lord was talking about this great day when we will all make it to Heaven. At least this was what I once thought. It never made sense to me why Jesus would want to save us so that we may join Him in Heaven, but leave us here waiting for this great day to arrive. This concept of the Kingdom remained unclear until God began to open my eyes to the truth of His Kingdom.

Think about this. The word "kingdom" was mentioned over 150 times in the New Testament, and at least 40 times in one of the Gospels alone. Jesus only mentioned the word church, "ecclesia" two times throughout the Gospel. Yet we have come to know more about being a church and having church more than we know about being in God's Kingdom. I do believe that a lack of understanding about the Kingdom of God has been the biggest tragedy of the church.

Not knowing about this truth has caused us to be more concerned about building churches instead of building the Kingdom. We have become extremely successful in building churches, ministries, and Christian organizations instead of advancing God's Kingdom. Not walking into the revelations of God's Kingdom has caused many people to become successful in the wrong assignments of life.

Knowing and living in God's Kingdom is the difference between living a religious life for the Lord and living a distinguished life. *"I must preach the kingdom of God to the other cities also, because for this purpose I have been sent" (Luke 4:43, NKJV)*. I would like to suggest that whatever the reason why Jesus was sent here into the world should also be the same reason why we are still in this world as believers. Let His purpose begin to become our purpose, and let's begin to center our lives on His Kingdom.

What Is This Kingdom

For starters, let's look at the Greek word "Basilea." This word is the message that Jesus and John the Baptist used as they proclaimed, *"Repent for the Kingdom of Heaven is at hand" (Matthew 4:17, NKJV)*. Basilea carries the meaning of the territory where a king's dominion, rule, and reign has been enforced. It is the realm where the king has the superior influence.

In fact, the word kingdom is a compound word, the king's domain. The king's domain is the area and territory where his power and influence has been enforced. Basilea speaks to a government that has been established by a king, and in this case, this King would be Jesus and this government was the Kingdom of Heaven. This truth means that of all the things that Jesus is, the one thing that we must embrace Him as is King. Not just any king, but the One in which "every knee will bow, and every tongue will confess" that Jesus is Lord and King.

When Jesus came on the scene, He wasn't coming to hold a church service, or simply entertain people with miracles. He wasn't coming just to give great sermons or teach people how to be "Christians." In essence, Jesus didn't come to build another religion, but instead He came to build a government. This government would be called the Kingdom of God. Many of the words that Jesus used to explain His Kingdom were more political in nature than they were religious.

For example, in *Matthew 16:18*, Jesus tells His disciples that *"and on this rock I will build My church."* The word used for "church" was "ecclesia." This word "ecclesia" had a more political meaning back then than it does today. The ecclesia was a "called out" group of citizens that were instrumental in assisting the king to enforce his reign throughout his kingdom. What a cabinet may be to the president of the United

States, is what the ecclesia was supposed to be to Jesus. We were to be a "called out," set apart group that was designated to enforce the works of Jesus and to build His Kingdom here on earth.

Because of the times that they were in and because of the kingdom of Rome at this time Jesus' disciple knew exactly what He was referring to by calling them His ecclesia. Because we have failed to understand the Kingdom of God we have relegated this word "ecclesia" to nothing more than a religious term. When you hear the word church, it is not abnormal for a picture of a building, a congregation and a service to pop up in your mind. These thing was not what Jesus had in mind.

When calling His disciples, and His followers today His church (ecclesia), He was saying that throughout His government we would be the individuals that He would use to enforce His dominion, power, rule and reign to the ends of the earth. We are those that God has chosen to serve with Him in the spreading of His Kingdom. *"The kingdoms of this world have become the kingdoms of our Lord" (Revelation 11:15, NKJV).* The Kingdom of God was God's original desire to spread His influence and reign from Heaven into the earth, causing this world to look like His. He has always desired to do this through us, His people!

Throughout Jesus' public ministry He showed us what this Kingdom of God would entail. To simplify the definition of this Kingdom of God, let's go to what has probably been known as the most famous prayer recorded throughout the Bible, "The Lord's Prayer." In this prayer, Jesus once again gives us such an accurate glimpse and a simple definition of the Kingdom. *"So He said to them, when you pray, say: Our Father in heaven, Hallowed be Your name. Your kingdom come. Your will be done On earth as it is in heaven" (Luke 11:2, NKJV).* Did you catch what He defined the Kingdom of God to be? Once again, He said, *"Your Kingdom come. Your will be done on earth as it is in Heaven."*

The Kingdom of God is simply seeing God's will done on earth as it is in Heaven. I do believe that God's desire was for this world to look just like His world, and for His rule to be extended from Heaven to earth. I believe this was evident when God made man in His image and placed him in the garden. The charge to *"tend the garden and keep it" (Genesis 2:15, NKJV)* and to *"Be fruitful and multiply; fill the earth and subdue it; have dominion..." (Genesis 1:28, NKJV)* over all of the creation was for man to spread this garden all over the earth. Just as the first Adam messed everything up, it was the "last Adam," Jesus, who came to restore this Heavenly rule and reign back to earth.

The centerpiece of this prayer is now our charge to be restored back to the original mandate that was given in the garden and to finish where Jesus' ministry on Earth left off. That is that we are to carry out His finished works, spread His Gospel, and enforce His dominion everywhere we go. When we join Him in this Kingdom work, we will begin to see God's will done on earth as we know it to be in Heaven. Others will begin to experience what it is like to have Heaven on earth. Learning to live distinguished now begins as we come to realize that our purpose here is to help usher in God's world into this one.

The significance of a kingdom is only defined and established by the value and the identity of its King. What makes this Kingdom any different from any other kingdom and government? Jesus! He is what makes the difference! Jesus is the "Lord of Lords and the King of Kings." This means that every lord or king that has or will ever exist will one day be subjected to King Jesus. The center of a Kingdom is its King and in order to be used to build and advance God's Kingdom, it is imperative that we acknowledge Jesus for who He truly is, the King of all creation.

From Heaven to Earth

The whole concept of practically experiencing God's will being done on earth as it is in Heaven at first may seem a little mystical. Then to hear that God wants to use you to do so really begins to sound far-fetched. As mystical or far-fetched as this may sound, it is absolutely true, and God is expecting us to learn how to live from Heaven to earth.

> *"I will give you the keys of the kingdom of heaven, and whatever you bind on earth will be bound in heaven, and whatever you loose on earth will be loosed in heaven" (Matthew 16:19, NKJV).*

The appropriate way to interpret this passage is that Jesus has given His followers the authority and power to allow on earth all of the great things that are taking place in Heaven. To disallow everything on earth that has been prohibited in Heaven. In other words, we have been deputized to recognize the climate and atmospheres of Heaven. Our job is to be led by God to cause the atmosphere of Heaven to become tangible and experienced in our everyday lives.

What does this look like? For a moment just imagine what all exists in Heaven: Healing, peace and wholeness exist in Heaven. No one in Heaven is sick or ill. Therefore, we have now been authorized and commissioned by God to "bind" and prohibit sickness to run rampant on earth and in the lives of others. Simply because God desires for us to experience Heaven here and now. There is provision, prosperity, and creative wisdom in Heaven. Therefore, we shall now expect to experience God's prosperity and creativity in our lives.

As we become more conscious of the Kingdom of Heaven, we will begin to reflect and carry the Kingdom into every environment. This is what Jesus did. As we read the stories and accounts of Jesus throughout the Gospels, let's begin to think of Jesus as Heaven on earth in the flesh. Everywhere Jesus went, the environment of Heaven was evident and made manifest. People could not remain sick while in His presence. Demons could no longer occupy the lives of others when He came around. Those who were oppressed by the legalistic laws of the land would now experience the goodness of God's grace. What was taking place at these times? Everything that was a reality within Heaven was then becoming a reality here on earth through the work and ministry of Jesus.

Jesus was the epitome of living a distinguished life from Heaven to earth. In fact, He gave us some insight on how this was done and how we are to do the same. *"No one has ascended to heaven but He who came down from heaven, that is, the Son of Man who is in heaven" (John 3:13, NKJV).* Jesus was telling Nicodemus that no one has seen Heaven except Him. Jesus was conscious of Heaven while still living here on earth. Jesus was used by His Father by way of the Holy Spirit to manifest the blessings of Heaven everywhere He went and in all that He did. Jesus lived simultaneously in two different worlds. His job was to bring one world into another one, and with His commission, He now expects us to do the same.

"Blessed be the God and Father of our Lord Jesus Christ, who has blessed us with every spiritual blessing in the heavenly places in Christ" (Ephesians 1:3, NKJV). In Jesus, our blessings are stored up in "heavenly places." They may originate in Heaven, but we are to experience God's blessings here on earth. We are expected to extend these Heavenly blessings into the lives of others as we advance God's Kingdom. *"And raised us up together, and made us sit together in the heavenly places in Christ Jesus" (Ephesians 2:6, NKJV).* These passages speak to the fact that in the Lord we are now able to be simultaneously aware of two different worlds.

According to Ephesians 2:6, we are now seated with Christ in Heavenly places. At some point, we should begin to reflect where we are seated. The Kingdom mandate of God to see His *"will be done on earth as it is in Heaven"* is accomplished as we begin to realize that we are called to live from Heaven to earth. The Kingdom of God is not about trying to fix this world and be the solution to all of this world's problems. Instead, the Kingdom of Heaven is all about replacing this world with His. It is now our responsibility to manifest the blessings, peace, healing, and wisdom of Heaven as we remain mindful of where God has seated us in the Lord.

Finding Our Purpose

At the heart of the Kingdom of God is this notion that God desires for His people not just to go out and witness, but to change the cultures of our societies. We are to point people to a more superior way of living and to build a tangible Kingdom culture right where we live. It is the revelation of the Kingdom that a believer comes to find his/her purpose. It is with the Kingdom where we begin to understand why He has given us a certain passion, talent, skill or ability. We are supposed to surrender these dreams and abilities back to God. In doing so, God will then lead us to how we are to build His Kingdom in our homes, campuses, communities and careers. Living a life of significance now becomes defined as we begin to enter and explore God's Kingdom. Living distinguished now meets its purpose and potential as we begin to understand God's plans for our lives.

The "Great Commission" is our purpose, but how God may plan for each of us to fulfill this commission will be different. For example, for the ones who have an absolute love for music, they should not think it strange that God has given them this natural musical proclivity. Their lives may be used to usher in God's Kingdom through music. For those who have a natural bending towards politics and to see justice prevail throughout our land, there is a purpose to fulfill in Jesus' commission. As they begin to come to the realization of God's Kingdom and His plans, God may use them to open doors for His Kingdom to invade the political realm.

Man-made religion has kept the purposes of God's people relegated to the church. Remember, it was Jesus' plans that the church would join Him to build His government. Man-made religion would say that every believer who has a beautiful voice should only glorify God with that voice during the Sunday services; otherwise, it would be considered blasphemy. When observing the life and career of the hit maker Mali Music and his venture into the secular realm of R&B music, I came to understand the Kingdom. It was at this point that I was confronted with either being bound by religious doctrines or liberated by the truth of Kingdom purpose. It wasn't that he was to keep his gift and message within the Gospel industry. Instead, God had led him to take this message into an industry that needed to know about His God and His message.

God is waiting for people to leave their traditions of man-made religion and join Him in His Kingdom work. Without the Kingdom, all of us will remain lost in what God's true plans and purposes are for our lives. As we begin to allow God's Spirit to bring us into the revelation of the Kingdom of God, life will begin to make more sense, our purposes will become more defined, and we will all become more effective in displaying the nature of our King, Jesus, in our everyday lives.

Kingdom Employment

God's Kingdom will never run out of purpose for His people. In fact, God never created us for a job, but He did create us for a purpose. We were never created to solely work a "9 to 5," but instead, we were created for God's assignments and plans wherever God may send us. I like what the late Dr. Myles Munroe once said, *"You can be fired from your job, but you can never be fired from your purpose."* Your purpose is the intent and reason why God has created you and why He has placed you where you are.

With this being said, I have seen too many of God's people spend their entire lives simply trying to find a job, work a job, try to make ends meet and hopefully work long enough to retire comfortably. As commendable as these plans may be, too many times this is our only aspiration in life. We fail to realize that God has commissioned us for a specific purpose. He may place us on a job to work with excellence, but we are never to confuse our jobs as being our purpose. Purpose may be on the job, but our jobs and our occupations are never to be our purposes by themselves. Why am I stressing this? Simply because God's Kingdom comes with a specific purpose. As we come to discover God's Kingdom, we will also come to discover God's Kingdom employment.

The success of our efforts on our jobs, careers, and places of employment may be contingent on our understanding of why God has placed us at that place. None of our steps are accidental. The Bible says, and I concur, that all of the steps of God's people are truly ordered by the Lord. He is intentional with guiding us to specific places with a commission, purpose, and plan from Him. If God's people were to develop this Kingdom mindset for employment, I am certain that the employment rate within the body of Christ would totally contradict the employment rate of this world. We would begin to reflect a culture of people who have become purpose driven for Kingdom employment.

So it is with living from Heaven to earth. There is no such thing as unemployment in the Kingdom of God because there is no such thing as unemployment in Heaven. There are only seasons of transition. Perhaps you may be between two jobs, the closing of one door of employment while waiting for another open door of employment. I would like to encourage you. You are not unemployed. Instead, you are in transition, and perhaps God is trying to give you marching orders for a new assignment.

Imagine the Kingdom as God's staffing agency. He has job placements for all of us. He knows our experiences with Him, the gifts that He has graced us with, the wisdom that He has endowed upon us, and the people who are in need of His Kingdom. Then He calls you up and says, *"I have a job for you. This company will be hiring you for this reason. I will bless you and cause you to excel. You are to touch the lives of others with my Kingdom and introduce them to me, the King. As you take care of my business, I will take care of your business."* If you could visualize this conversation with God, then you will also come to grasp the concept of Kingdom employment.

Remember the charge and purpose of the Kingdom; that God's *"will may be done on earth as it is in Heaven."* As you begin to enter into your jobs, careers, or even your school campuses, just know that God will use you to change the environments of these places by bringing Heaven with you in all that you do. As you are joining God in his work, you will be one of the ones to add value to where you are. You will become an asset to your company instead of a liability. You will be known as the one that others like to be around simply because of His presence that comes along with you. It was Joseph whom the Bible says that the "Lord was with him, and he was successful." This is the goal and the result of being employed by the King and being used to build God's Kingdom, even in your place of employment.

Kingdom Economics

In relation to being employed by God's Kingdom, we must know that our live-lihoods are provided for by God. It is imperative that we recognize that it is His Kingdom that shall provide all of our needs. Jesus has now restored us back to the original plans of God before the fall of Adam and Eve. I'd like to believe that the Garden of Eden was symbolic of the Kingdom of God.

Let's think for a moment what life was like in the Garden of Eden so we may have a better understanding of what living in God's Kingdom shall be like for us now. Before the fall, man did not have a job; he only had a purpose. Man was able to walk with God while in the garden. Man didn't have to work or toil for His own food, livelihood, or existence as we have to do today. Everything that Adam and Eve would need was provided for them by God in the garden. All they had to do was be concerned with being "blessed, being fruitful, multiplying, subduing the earth, (Genesis 1:28) and enforcing God's dominion."

Listen to the curse that was pronounced on humanity as a result of Adam and Eve's sin. *"Cursed is the ground for your sake; In toil you shall eat of it. All the days of your life" (Genesis 3:17, NKJV).* The food, livelihood and existence that was once provided for by God, Adam would now have to obtain through work. It is not a curse to have a mindset to work to maintain a living for yourself and your family but toiling to work is where the curse lies.

Jesus took upon Himself the curse of sin that so that we are now restored back to the original Kingdom order of living before the fall. In other words, because of Jesus and as we learn to live within His Kingdom, we no longer need to "toil" and work to live an abundant life in the Lord. In fact, Jesus tells those who were fol-lowing Him to *"not work for food that spoils, but for food that endures to eternal life" (John 6:27, NIV).*

Even when Simon would begin to tell Jesus about his frustrated night of fishing, he tells Jesus *"we have toiled all night and caught nothing" (Luke 5:5, NKJV).* I would suggest that he had to work in order to eat. As Jesus was on his boat, He began to introduce Simon to the Kingdom of God where man doesn't have to toil to eat as long as they are in His Kingdom. Simon's blessing could not be worked for but only caught and received as Jesus, and His Kingdom had invaded His boat. Jesus showed Simon what it was like for Adam and Eve in the Garden of Eden before their fall. He was introducing Simon to a new system, a new way of living; the Kingdom of God!

What does this mean for us today? If we desire to join God in His Kingdom work and to understand Kingdom employment, we must also understand that our work and labor shall never be simply to maintain a living, survive or exist in life. Our existence can never be contingent on our labor and work. Rather, when we do work, it is always for God's Kingdom purposes. It is always to see the Kingdom of God advance wherever He has placed us.

It has become all too normal for our decision-making process for our job placement to be contingent on the hours, pay, wages, and benefits. As great as these things may be they should not be the determining factors in where we will serve. Instead, it must be where God needs us to be and who the people are that He is calling us to. In the Kingdom, our blessings and livelihood will not be dependent upon the amount of hours that we work, our wages or the overtime that is being offered. Our work in His kingdom will always be to see His will being done, and it is His will that all of our needs shall be met in the Lord.

Conducting Kingdom Business

As Jesus was preparing His disciples, He would give them a parable with the intention of teaching them the ways of His Kingdom. Jesus gave them specific instructions to follow after His death, burial and resurrection. *"And he called his ten servants, and delivered them ten pounds, and said unto them, occupy till I come"* *(Luke 19:13, KJV)*. He calls them to occupy the land, but the NKJV gives us some more insight into these instructions. *"So he called ten of his servants, delivered to them ten minas, and said to them, 'Do business till I come"* *(Luke 19:13, NKJV)*. After He would leave them and eventually send His Spirit to fill them, the work of His Kingdom was to continue to go on with His disciples.

This work was the enforcing of His finished works, and the disciples were called to conduct Kingdom business on behalf of the resurrected King! What is this Kingdom business that we are to be conducting? To "occupy the land" and to "do His business." To carry out His finished works and to enforce the victory that was won at the Cross in everything that we do.

The engaging of this Kingdom business is to fulfill His "Great Commission". We have been called to spread His Gospel in word and deed. We are called to baptize others in His name, and to teach them the ways of the Kingdom by sharing our lives with them. We are to make disciples of the Lord and guide others on how to be His representatives in this world. What other business would you fill up your schedule within the world that is greater than His Kingdom business? He has called us to steward this call faithfully and to join Him in His work.

Let's allow God to begin to guide us in conducting His Kingdom business. As we submit our plans to God, we will all begin to see His plans for the Kingdom become unveiled before our very eyes. We will begin to feel our hearts swell up with the revelation of His will made known to us. We will become fueled with passion and excitement as the dots begin to connect between why we are here and how we can be used to reconcile others back to God.

Every day that you desire to do the work of the Kingdom you can expect spiritual warfare and attacks from the enemy. Like the men that were rebuilding the walls of Israel with Nehemiah, we should never drop our tools, just to pick up our weapons (Nehemiah 4:17). Instead, we must realize that as Kingdom citizens we are now on offense. We are to move forward in conducting Kingdom business. It was Joshua who encouraged the Israelites to *"go and possess the land" (Joshua 18:3)*. Every time the enemy attacked God's people, it was because they were moving forward into new territory. Let's do just that. Let's "go and possess the land," and "occupy till He returns" as we follow God's leading in the building of His Kingdom.

Infiltrating Systems

We have been commissioned by the Lord to spread the influence of God's kingdom throughout this world. As true followers of Jesus, we should have more of an impact and influence on the world, than the world having an impact on us. One aspect of the Kingdom is that it points to a more superior way of living in the Lord. As the people around the world get a glimpse of the Kingdom way of living, it will only be a matter of time before they will begin to seek out the King.

The principles of the Kingdom will always point others to the presence of the King! How will others come to know of God's principles and presence? It is as we surrender our lives unto the Lord, and not just enter into His Kingdom, but even more, allow His Kingdom to enter into us. It was the mission of Adam and Eve to "tend the garden" and to spread the garden everywhere they went. This assignment is true with us as we follow God's leading and go into the various systems of this world.

When I mention this word "system," I mean it as being the various sets of structures in which this world has depended on to make a living and to thrive in life. These systems have been the structures of our society that have governed the way we think, the way we live, and the way that we have come to see life. Just as God has a plan for these systems so that His rule and reign may prevail within this world, so does Satan.

Spiritually today the kingdoms of this world are considered the systems of this world. Whoever is in control of these systems will ultimately spread their influence throughout this world. Knowing this, God has called us to infiltrate these systems and to spread His Kingdom influence throughout these kingdoms. God has called us to go and possess and occupy these systems for His glory. No longer is the land of Canaan the land that we are to go into and possess. Instead, it is the various systems and kingdoms of this world. Let's briefly mention what a few of these systems are.

These systems consist of the community structures of family, and if you have noticed the enemy has launched an onslaught of attacks against our families with the hope of dividing. Our communities are only as strong as our families, and it is a "house that is divided that will never stand." Therefore, God has called the family of God to stand for righteousness and rebuild our homes and communities by building His Kingdom one family at a time. God is raising up Godly marriages, children, men and women who will join Him in His work to redefine the definitions of family and restore our communities back to the ways of God.

One system and structure of this world is also the realm of politics. If there were ever a system that needs the ways of righteousness to infiltrate it, this would be that one system. With all of the corruption, fraudulent and compromised politics and politicians, we must be reminded that *"Righteousness exalts a nation" (Proverbs 14:34, NKJV)*. One problem that has plagued many of God's people is that we have been placing our trust in the wrong government. We have been expecting the governments of this world and our nation to do only what God's government is capable of doing. That is saving and making this world right again. All of the wrongs that we have seen in this system of politics is designed to point us to all that is right in God's Kingdom.

The various industries of music, arts, sports, and entertainment would be another system and structure within this world that is up for grabs. For too long we have seen these systems polluted with immorality. Whoever is in charge of these systems is the one who governs the lives that are subjected to these systems. Satan, who has been known as the "prince of the power of the air," (Ephesians 2:2), has traditionally been the one who has controlled this system. With all of the gifts, talents, passion and Kingdom ambition that God has placed within this generation, we are now seeing a powerful move of God that is rising up within this particular kingdom. This is with the intent of seeing God's Kingdom infiltrate the airways and begin to change what we think, how we live, how we see life, and to point others to the soon coming King.

There are many other systems in which God is raising up His people to bring Heaven into this world. Other systems like business, media, education, religion and the healthcare systems of this world. Jesus best illustrated this as He gave His disciples another parable of the Kingdom.

> *"Another parable He spoke to them: "The kingdom of heaven is like leaven, which a woman took and hid in three measures of meal till it was all leavened" (Matthew 13:33, NKJV).*

First off, the Kingdom resembled a little bit of leaven that a woman took and "hid" in the dough. It's key that we see the influence of the Kingdom of God even when it is hidden. The Kingdom of God doesn't have to be out front, or be the supervisor on the job, or even be the pastor of the church. The power, authority and influence of the Kingdom can be the humble employee who comes in and does his/her job. They come into the workplace letting their "light so shine before others." Not broadcasting the Gospel, but rather living it out before their peers. Before you know it, their influence of the Kingdom has spread throughout the whole company, and the very presence of the King has been embraced. The Holman Christian Study Bible says that the woman "mixed" the leaven into the dough. This is just like God to find someone who is willing to conduct his Kingdom business and mix them into our society, and empower them to spread His Kingdom influence everywhere He would lead them.

Lastly, we see that this little bit of leaven that was initially hidden would eventually take over the entire lump of dough until "it was all leavened." The mission of the Kingdom is that wherever it goes and takes residence that it will eventually take over until all of the systems of this world will begin to look like the Kingdom of our God. The Kingdom of God has not come to earth in order to fix these systems or structures of our society. Instead, the Kingdom is here to replace these systems with God's Kingdom. It is here to point others to a more superior way of living.

God desires that through every structure of our society, people may experience His Heaven on earth and the goodness of our King! Let's no longer idly stand by and watch the enemy occupy the systems of this world that we have been commissioned to infiltrate and take over for the Lord. Let's get onboard with the commission of the King, serve as true ambassadors of Christ and live a distinguished life in the Lord.

Building God's Government

I want to end this chapter as I first started it. That is getting back to the concept of the Kingdom as God's government. Being God's people, the church, we are the ones who have been assigned to build God's government here on earth. We are the ones that God desires to make the difference for His Kingdom.

> *"For unto us a Child is born, unto us a Son is given; and the government will be upon His shoulder. And His name will be called Wonderful, Counselor, Mighty God, Everlasting Father, Prince of Peace. Of the increase of His government and peace. There will be no end" (Isaiah 9:6-7, NKJV).*

Let's examine this passage for a moment. The Prophet Isaiah tells us how this government shall come about here on earth. He says, "The government will be upon His shoulders." What are the shoulders an intricate part of? They are a part of one's body. Whose body is this in reference of? This passage is referencing the body of Jesus. Therefore, in essence, the prophet was telling us that it is the body of Christ that Jesus' government and Kingdom shall be carried upon and resting on.

God desires that the governments of this world would rest upon Him. It is at this hour of the Kingdom that God is raising up government leaders and political figures who are after His own heart. With this being said, the governments, and policies of this world were never where our trust was supposed to be. Our trust was always supposed to be in God and His Kingdom. Being God's people, this is the government that God has chosen us to advance throughout the earth.

This truth is important to be conscious of because if we are not mindful of this fact, we will become consumed with building the wrong things in life hoping that they will be the solution to this world's problems. You have been called to a highly ranking position in God's government so that your life may serve as a representation of Him. God has called you to conduct His business and live out His Kingdom purposes in this world. Let's get back to work as we will dedicate our lives to the commission of God to see Heaven invade earth and to see His government reign in all areas of our lives.

Living A Kingdom Lifestyle

When it is all said and done, the Kingdom isn't a religion. It is not a set of ritualistic rules and traditions. The Kingdom is a government, and it is God's will being done. At the end of the day, the Kingdom of God is a lifestyle. It is a way of living, doing life, and thriving in life. The call to the Kingdom is a call to reign with the Lord.

> *"Much more those who receive abundance of grace and of the gift of righteousness will reign in life through the One, Jesus Christ"* *(Romans 5:17, NKJV).*

To reign in life is to live a triumphant life above the calamities of this world. It is to live in victory over sin, and all of the effects of sin. Living in the Kingdom is to have a glow about your life and a certain countenance of confidence, victory and expectation in the Lord. The Kingdom would be reflected in the life of the person who is not subjected to the ways of this world. They are in this world, but not of this world. They have entered into God's Kingdom, and God's way of living life.

The ways of this world and all of its limitations will not define, limit nor hold them down. I want to encourage you that today you can be this person. You can be that Kingdom representative and ambassador for Christ, representing Him before the world. A lifestyle of abundance, victory and blessings await you, and it is one heartfelt decision away. Will you enter into His Kingdom or stand on the outside and watch? To live distinguished is to live a Kingdom lifestyle.

When we come to realize all that we need in this life is in Jesus, we will never have to spend another moment seeking anything other than Him to achieve our purposes. In Christ, you now have "all things that pertain to life and Godliness." I am excited for the life, journey and path of greatness that lies ahead of you. Your tomorrow will be different than your today, and each day with Jesus will be better than the day before. So what are we waiting on? Let's go, and let's fulfill what we were created for in God. Let's live a distinguished life in the Lord! Let us leave our fingerprint on the world!

Acknowledgment

Heavenly Father, you have revealed yourself to the world through your Son, Jesus Christ. Use this book to spread your gospel truth around the world. Reconcile your people and raise up disciples for your Kingdom. Rekindle the fire within the hearts of men for a more intimate relationship with you. Bring fresh encounters, personal and corporate revival to all men. In Jesus Name, Amen!

To our parents, *Shelia Payne* and *James Greene*, thank you for developing a foundation for us to know God for ourselves.

To our Pastor and First Lady, *Bishop Joseph W. Walker, III*, and *Dr. Stephaine Walker*, thank you for your leadership and support.

To our editing angel, *Rita Quarles*. Thank you so much for your work. God bless you!

To all of our friends, family, and loved ones. Thank you for your love, prayers, and support.

To our co-laborers in prayer, the Mount Zion Prayer Ministry. Thank you for your continuous prayers and for simply living life with us.

To our CBN family. Thank you for continuing to show us what God's Kingdom looks like, day in and day out. God bless you!"

CPSIA information can be obtained
at www.ICGtesting.com
Printed in the USA
LVOW04s0911030916
502868LV00021B/28/P

9 781498 481748